PERGAMON GENERAL PSYCHOLOGY SERIES

Editors: Arnold P. Goldstein, *Syracuse University*
Leonard Krasner, *SUNY, Stony Brook*

A Guide to
Behavioral Analysis
and Therapy

PGPS-19

A Guide to Behavioral Analysis and Therapy

Robert Paul Liberman, M.D.
Research Psychiatrist
Center for the Study of Behavioral Disorders
Camarillo State Hospital, Camarillo, California
and
Assistant Clinical Professor of Psychiatry
U.C.L.A. School of Medicine

PERGAMON PRESS INC.

New York · Toronto · Oxford · Sydney · Braunschweig

PERGAMON PRESS INC.
Maxwell House, Fairview Park, Elmsford, N.Y. 10523

PERGAMON OF CANADA LTD.
207 Queen's Quay West, Toronto 117, Ontario

PERGAMON PRESS LTD.
Headington Hill Hall, Oxford

PERGAMON PRESS (AUST.) PTY. LTD.
Rushcutters Bay, Sydney, N.S.W.

VIEWEG & SOHN GmbH
Burgplatz 1, Braunschweig

Printed in the United States of America

08 016645 8 (H)
08 016786 1 (S)

To Gertrude and Harry who know how to reinforce behavior with love

CONTENTS

FOREWORD

The field of psychiatry is presently in a state of major transition. It has been a discipline constrained by an imperfect body of theory, and by a relatively limited range of therapies. Today there is a new and refreshing wind blowing across our musty desks, couches, and clinics. The outline of a revitalized profession can be seen emerging from clouds of dust churned up by vigorous plowing in a number of promising new fields. One of the most active of these fields, with rich soil and fast-growing crops, is that of behavior therapy.

The term "behavior therapy" is not an attractive one. It has overtones of operant conditioning (suggestive of animal learning experiments rather than help for people in trouble). Perhaps this general approach will eventually be called psychotherapeutically programmed affective re-education—but I doubt it. What's important is that we find a growing body of data supporting the effectiveness of a method that is fairly consistent from one laboratory and one clinic to another.

Now, thanks to Dr. Liberman's efforts, we have a well-organized, lucid, and highly usable manual of instruction for the prospective behavior therapist, regardless of his background.

Psychiatry has not been distinguished in bringing forward new ideas and techniques designed to help large numbers of people. Psychiatrists are cautious about adopting new treatments—in most cases, rightly so—but this has caused delays in adopting innovative procedures over the past century. Since Pinel removed the chains from patients in the Paris Bicêtre in 1792, there have been relatively few major advances in the treatment of mental illness. Psychiatry has had to be content with largely traditional methods of diagnosis and treatment. Psychoanalysis, shock treatments, tranquilizing drugs, and group psychotherapy are among the few really useful developments of the last 75 years. Only recently has a move begun away from traditional ways of *viewing* mental illness, and from the accepted practice of treating mentally ill patients in a custodial setting isolated from the rest of the community.

Behavioral therapy, originally developed by psychologists and rooted in both Pavlovian and operant learning theory, made its first appearance on the mental health scene in 1924 when Mary Cover Jones worked out her method of "counter-conditioning." This, like Couéism, enjoyed a brief vogue, and then for all practical purposes disappeared from the psychotherapeutic scene. Thirty years later Joseph Wolpe worked out his method of "desensitization" along very much the same lines. In the meantime B. F. Skinner and his colleagues at Harvard had begun (in the late 1940's) to apply learning theory to psychotherapy. During the next two decades much more work was done at

Harvard by Skinner and his students, one of whom (Ogden Lindsley) pioneered the use of operant methods with severely psychotic, chronically hospitalized patients. More recently at the Neuropsychiatric Institute at UCLA, O. I. Lovaas and J. Q. Simmons applied the principles of operant conditioning to the development of speech and other adaptive behaviors in autistic children.

Behavior modification in clinical practice has given rise to theoretical arguments which are still raging among its adherents and opponents. The role of suggestion in the effectiveness of the treatment has not yet been adequately determined. Nor has it been learned how a treatment based on relieving the patient's symptoms rather than on eliminating the causes of his disturbance will be effective over a long post-treatment period.

However, practitioners of the healing arts have always striven to relieve symptoms, even when their basic causes could be neither discovered nor changed. Taboos against techniques based on the treatment of symptoms alone have held psychiatrists back from accepting new methods of treatment for too long. One virtue of Dr. Liberman's book is that it does not attempt to offer any final answers to these questions. It simply and clearly explains what behavioral modification means and how the technique can be applied.

Dr. Liberman has given us a training manual for the application of techniques of behavioral modification, ingeniously presented in the form of programmed instruction. This will give health workers who are neither psychiatrists nor psychologists a method with which, under proper supervision, they may be able to alleviate symptoms of maladaptive behavior in less time-consuming and less expensive ways. At the same time, this book will be welcomed by psychiatrists and psychologists, because it points out a way in which they and their co-workers may be able to understand and employ behavior modification as a clinically useful technique.

University of California,   Louis Jolyon West, M.D.
Los Angeles, California

INTRODUCTION

Behavior therapy is an exciting new development in the mental health universe. But what does behavior therapy consist of and what does it amount to? This book is for people who wish to acquaint themselves with the growing field of behavior therapy, to understand the basic principles of learning which serve as its foundation, and to become familiar with some of its clinical applications.

The literature on behavior therapy is vast and growing at an exponential rate. Most individuals, both professional and lay, however, do not have the time or energy to work through the numerous journal articles and books which deal with the subject. I have written this book so that interested people can obtain a comprehensive introduction to what behavior therapy is in a quick way. The reader should be able to finish the book within three hours and should be encouraged to read parts of it at a time. It is the kind of book that can be left at the bedside or bathside for periodic openings and closings.

The people who can make use of this book are:

1. Practicing mental health clinicians, such as psychiatrists, psychologists, social workers, nurses, aides, occupational and recreational therapists, who want a quick introduction to the field and some suggestions on how to learn more about behavior therapy in the future;
2. Psychotherapists who are curious about adding some new and effective techniques to their repertoires;
3. Teachers and school counselors who want to find out more about the behavioral approach to improving classroom control and academic performance;
4. Interested lay people who have heard about behavior therapy and want to learn more about it;
5. Individuals who have specific behavioral problems themselves or with their children and are seeking new ways of looking at them.

The book is primarily oriented toward giving the reader an intellectual understanding of behavior therapy and whetting his appetite for learning to use the techniques through more intensive training. From this point of view, the book tells "what it's about" rather than "how to do it." Some readers—particularly more adventurous clinicians—may obtain enough information from the book to begin trying out the methods on their own. However, supervision and further training is strongly recommended for those who want to give behavior therapy a fair clinical trial.

A wide range of human behavior is covered by the book, including the problems of the hospitalized patient, the functioning but suffering neurotic with anxiety or depression, the juvenile delinquent, the hyperactive child, and the retardate. Many types of deviant behavior which have been successfully dealt with by behavior therapists could not be included in this brief book and the interested reader should refer to the Annotated Bibliography at the end of the book for additional information. The problem behaviors chosen for this book do represent, however, the major applications of behavior therapy to date.

The first part of the book introduces the reader to the basic principles of learning from which behavior therapy techniques are developed. I have attempted to avoid burdening the reader with a pedantic or academic presentation, instead relying mostly on practical and concrete vignettes to illustrate the basic principles. The reader can utilize his assimilation of the basic principles in Part Two of the book when he reads about how behavior therapy is applied.

At various places in the text, the reader is asked a question and given a chance to respond using the information he has gained. He is also told whether his answer is correct or not with additional clarification of the material involved. This "semi-programmed" format is used because it gives the reader a direct opportunity to experience his own behavior under the influence of learning principles. The feedback that the reader obtains by checking his answers should give him a feeling for "reinforcement," one of the prime principles governing behavior. As the reader proceeds through the book, he will gain gradually increasing competence in understanding behavior therapy thereby experiencing another behavior principle, called "shaping."

This book has been three years in the making. I decided to write it when I was being exposed to behavior therapy myself for the first time as a psychiatric resident. There was no simple and direct source that existed (or exists today) for a rapid introduction to the field. I hope that my effort to bring behavior therapy to a large number of curious but busy professionals in the mental health field reaches its behavioral goal. I welcome any reactions to the book and hope to periodically up-date it.

ROBERT P. LIBERMAN, M.D.

ACKNOWLEDGEMENTS

I appreciate the professional assistance rendered to me by my editorial associate, Lee Liberman, who had a hand in each phase of the manuscript from its conception on the beaches of St. John in the Virgin Islands to its final form. She has helped me use the English language in a more effective way and has helped me clarify my ideas.

With pleasure and nostalgia I thank my friends who brought the light of behavior therapy into my career—Lee Birk and David Shapiro. Also vital to this enterprise are those colleagues of mine who have served as models and reinforcers for my interest and work in behavior therapy—Harold Weiner, Daniel Brown, Halmuth Schaefer, John Paul Brady, Elliot Mishler, and B. F. Skinner. I am grateful for the helpful criticisms of my manuscript by Aaron T. Beck, Martin Denker and many others and for the encouragement by Leonard Krasner which led to its publication.

NOTE

This book has been written so that people may be able to introduce themselves to behavior therapy quickly but comprehensively. On many of the pages you will be asked a question. At these points, select the best answer and then turn to the page number designated to see whether or not you are right. The book will guide you through the material, giving you feedback on your accumulating knowledge of behavior therapy. It is this feedback process that forms the basis of much of behavior therapy, with patients obtaining clear and explicit reactions reflecting their progress. Thus, your experience of reading this book will give you a feeling for the process of behavior therapy.

You will not miss any crucial information by skipping the pages which indicate that a wrong answer has been made. However, you will probably find additional clarification of the material if you skim through the pages which give feedback on wrong answers. If you feel unsure of your knowledge at certain junctures, it might be advisable for you to read through all the possible answers to a question, but only after you have tried to pick the correct answer.

Sometimes you will find information presented on a left-hand page of this book (even numbered pages). This is supplementary material which you will find interesting and useful and which expands on the topics presented on the right-hand pages (odd numbered pages).

All the case examples given in this book are accounts of actual cases either treated by the author or excerpted from the published literature. Names and identifying characteristics have been altered to insure anonymity.

Part I

Basic Principles of Behavior

Chapter 1: THINKING BEHAVIORALLY ABOUT PSYCHIATRIC PROBLEMS

Behavior therapy begins by getting to know the patient as a person through a detailed and specific taking of a history and a discussion of the presenting problem. The therapist's first behavioral task is to identify the problem as a set of acts—to translate the psychopathology into precise, observable units of behavior. Behavior can consist of bodily movements, facial expressions, written or spoken language, and physiological responses.

A unit of behavior may encompass many successive acts such as: "Tony bangs his head against the floor, runs outside, takes off his clothes, and screams for his mother through the window." It would not help in specifying Tony's problem to say, "Tony had a temper tantrum." What distinguishes behavioral units is that they can be objectively and reliably observed, recorded, and described by different people. In the behavioral approach, an observer looks at and listens to human behavior without making assumptions and inferences about "internal" and hidden motivations.

Which of the following statements describes a clinical problem in basic, behavioral units?

Mrs. Jones has had an agoraphobia for five years . . . . turn to page 5.

Mrs. Jones is unable to go more than one block from her home without being accompanied by a relative. . . . . turn to page 7.

Mrs. Jones is an oral-dependent woman with fears of going outside alone . . . . turn to page 9.

You said that the statement, "Mrs. Jones has had an agoraphobia for five years," is phrased in basic behavioral units. This answer is incorrect because the key term, "agoraphobia," is a general, diagnostic label which does not *clearly specify* Mrs. Jones' incapacity. Is she unable to travel to the country? Is she unable to walk in the streets? Is she only restricted from going to distant cities, or to sports arenas? The statement does not tell us. For behavior therapy to proceed we must know exactly what the patient can or cannot do, does or doesn't do. We want to know under what conditions the patient is incapacitated. We must know the specific interpersonal and physical dimensions of the setting in which the problem occurs.

Let us try another behavioral problem. Mr. Grant, a chronically psychotic patient who has been hospitalized for ten years, is of interest to the staff on his ward because of his delightful word salad. He is able to produce the most fascinating neologisms, many of which seem to have psychosexual symbolism imbedded in them. Which of these statements might behaviorally describe Mr. Grant's symptomatology?

Mr. Grant's thought disorder includes references to people and monsters that seek to devour him, reflecting his oral fixation and his use of projection as a defense mechanism.................................... turn to page 11.

Mr. Grant talks about people and monsters that seek to devour him when he is in the presence of nurses and attendants on the ward, but rarely when he is alone... turn to page 13.

Clear, concise descriptions of human behavior have been given by astute observers since the painters depicting life among the cave-dwellers. The following extract is an example of a graphic behavioral description by the famous psychoanalyst, Wilhelm Reich, in *Character analysis*:

> The hysterical character (has as) its most outstanding characteristic an obvious sexual behavior, in combination with a specific kind of bodily agility with a definitely sexual nuance. . . . In women, the hysterical character type is evidenced by disguised or undisguised coquetry in gait, gaze and speech. In men, there is, in addition, softness and over-politeness, feminine facial expression and feminine behavior. . . . In the typical case, the movements are soft, more or less rolling, and sexually provocative.*

* Reprinted with permission of Farrar, Straus & Giroux, Inc., New York, from Wilhelm Reich's *Character analysis*. Copyright © 1949 by Noonday Press, Farrar, Straus & Giroux.

You picked the second statement as more behaviorally distinct. Correct! Knowing the geographic boundaries of Mrs. Jones' phobia as well as the interpersonal qualification associated with it gives us a good start in making a behavioral analysis of her problems.

Continue by turning to page 19, unless you want more practice in making behavioral descriptions. Two more case examples can be found on the bottom of pages 5 and 13.

You said that the statement, "Mrs. Jones is an oral-dependent woman with fears of going outside alone," is a good behavioral description of the patient's malady. Unfortunately, the terms, "oral-dependent" and "fears", are labels which impute meanings to Mrs. Jones' behavior that are difficult to verify. Moreover, they do not tell us what the patient's *specific* behavioral lacks are. Making a behavioral diagnosis is different from interpreting behavior as having unseen and unproven referents. Our task is to describe, not infer.

Return to the beginning and after re-reading the page, choose another answer.

You are making unnecessary assumptions about the meaning of Mr. Grant's problem. The question asks you for a description of the patient's symptomatology. The question does not ask you to speculate on the meaning of the symptom.

As we shall see shortly, verbalizations can be shaped and encouraged by factors external to the person's inner mental processes. In Mr. Grant's case, the staff which pays exceptional attention to his neologisms may be exerting a powerful influence on what he says. Mr. Grant may or may not be orally fixated, and may or may not have a thought disorder. By using these terms you describe events that allegedly occur remote in time or under the skin. In neither place can we be sure to make reliable observations.

Go back to page 5, read the material again and choose the correct answer.

You are catching on to the concept of behavior. The second statement reliably describes Mr. Grant's verbal behavior on the ward. It takes little or no inference to make that observation and it gives us important information on the interpersonal setting in which Mr. Grant's irrational talk occurs.

Let's go through one more example just to give you some added confidence in discern behavior.

Behavior is any action of an individual that can be objectively observed. Behavioral observation does not include interpretation of motives; we do not attribute intent to an individual's action but rather describe what the person is *doing*. Which of the following statements represents accurate behavioral description?

That patient pacing in the corner seems hostile and is hallucinating........
....turn to page 17.

That patient pacing in the corner is frowning and talking to himself........
....turn to page 15.

You picked the statement, "That patient pacing in the corner is frowning and talking to himself," as the accurate description of behavior. You are right. The statement consists of observations that many different people could agree upon. Making reliable descriptions of behavior is the important first step in our successful work with patients.

Turn to page 19.

When you state that the "patient . . . seems hostile and is hallucinating," you are inferring affect and behavior that is not easily verifiable. The patient indeed may be hostile and may be hallucinating but if we see him only frowning and talking out loud without anyone near him we require more details before drawing such a conclusion. To reliably describe him as "hostile and hallucinating" we would have to carry out further observations such as interviewing him or watching him for additional behavioral evidence.

Go back to page 13 and pick the correct answer.

Behavioral clinicians are interested in what patients *do* rather than in what they *are*. One individual might be described thus, "Max is schizophrenic," and another, "Minnie is really upset today." But we are interested in knowing what Max does that makes him viewed as a schizophrenic and what Minnie is doing that earns her the description "upset." Words such as "schizophrenic," "upset," "compulsive," or "mentally retarded" are summary statements referring to a large class of behaviors. It is frequently useful to employ such summaries, but not unless we have some common understanding of the specific, component behaviors to which they refer.

Spoken words are behaviors; in fact, language or verbal behavior makes up the most important portion of human behavior. Most psychotherapy focuses on verbal behavior—changes in patients' self-reports provide the usual assessment of clinical change. Later we will see how psychotherapy, as it is usually practiced by psychodynamically-oriented therapists, consists of a special type of learning mediated by verbal conditioning and modeling.

One task of any therapist is to sensitively identify various verbal responses as being concordant or discordant with what the therapist observes in the patient's non-verbal behavior. The clinical term, *inappropriate affect*, frequently refers to a disjunction between what a patient says and how he says it. A well-taken mental status examination is an example of clear and reliable behavioral assessment. Picture yourself evaluating the speech of a female patient and choose the statement which provides a better description of her verbal behavior:

The patient talked as though she were depressed...........turn to page 21.

The patient spoke slowly and in a monotone and stopped several times to sob... turn to page 23.

You said that the statement, "The patient talked as though she were depressed," provides a good description of verbal behavior.

Well, let's ask the key question. What will the patient be *doing* when she is depressed? Answering this question points us in the right direction.

Go back to page 19 and try again.

Extract by Charles Darwin, in *The expression of the emotions in man and animals*:

> Persons suffering from excessive and prolonged grief remain motionless and passive, or may occasionally rock themselves to and fro. The face becomes pale; the muscles flaccid; the eyelids droop; the head hangs on the contracted chest; the lips, cheeks, and lower jaw all sink downwards from their own weight. Hence all the features are lengthened; and the face of a person who bears bad news is said to fall. . . . After prolonged suffering the eyes become dull and lack expression, and are often slightly suffused with tears. The eyebrows not rarely are rendered oblique, which is due to their inner ends being raised. This produces peculiarly-formed wrinkles on the forehead, which are very different from those of a simple frown. The corners of the mouth are drawn downwards, which is so universally recognized as a sign of being out of spirits, that it is almost proverbial.*

We will see the importance of specifying non-verbal, emotional behavior in Chapter 10 where assertive training is described. Emotionally expressive behavior can be learned in therapy more efficiently when it is clearly targeted and defined.

---

* Reprinted with permission of The University of Chicago Press, Chicago, Illinois, from Charles Darwin's *The expression of the emotions in man and animals*.

Your choice of the second statement is right. It takes little in the way of inference to build a reliable picture of this patient. Several independent observers could easily agree on this type of description.

Thus we see that affects are also behaviors and that we can describe affects accurately and reliably by referring to their observable, behavioral components. Darwin utilized this method when he wrote *The expression of the emotions in man and animals*, and correlated the details of facial expression and body movement with emotions such as rage, fear, grief, and pleasure.

The key to a behavioral analysis of emotions lies in asking the question: "What is the person *doing* when he experiences the emotion?" Our interest is in facial expression, motor movements, vocalizations and speech. We are also interested in the physical and interpersonal environment—the setting in which the behavior occurs—especially the responses made by others to the person experiencing the emotion. Under certain conditions we may want to measure "under-the-skin" behaviors such as blood pressure, pulse rate, and galvanic skin response.

Mrs. Eaton, after seven years of psychodynamic psychotherapy and little symptomatic improvement, is terminated by her therapist and referred for behavior therapy. She articulately presents her problem as being one of "anxiety" whenever she is left alone. She insists that she has been unable to perform her duties as wife and mother without the presence of her husband or another of her relatives. When asked to describe what she experiences during times of anxiety, she hesitates but then lists phrases that are psychodynamic interpretations and elaborations of her problem. As though by rote memory, she discusses her unsatisfactory relationship with her mother and her envy of an older brother. When she is reminded that she hasn't described her subjective experience of anxiety, she says, "Dr. Paul says I'm afraid of losing control of myself." While talking about her incapacities, Mrs. Eaton shows little discomfort and appears quite relaxed. Further investigation reveals that her husband, in sympathetic concern over her well-being, has never permitted her to be alone or perform on her own during the past eight years. He has sacrificed his own pleasures and diversions to keep his wife company and to accompany her on shopping trips and family visits.

This vignette demonstrates how "talk about anxiety" can be a problem behavior by itself maintaining the patient in a dependent and "sick" role. Mrs. Eaton may or may not exhibit signs of anxiety when alone. The crucial fact is that her talking about it has extremely significant consequences—she is able to have her husband with her constantly, as well as the continuous concern of her therapist.

The stereotype of behavior therapy is that it deals only with surface, motor behavior—not with affects. I hope to put this stereotype to rest. For example, emotions that behavior therapists have dealt with are anger and hostility, anxiety and fear, assertiveness, self-destructiveness, craving for drugs and alcohol, sexual frigidity, impotence, sexual perversions, and affectionate responses.

Systematic desensitization, one of the major behavioral techniques, deals directly with the affect, "anxiety." Of course we must differentiate "anxiety" and its observable referents—tremulousness, sweating, palpitations, blushing and blanching, muscular tension, changes in the galvanic skin response—from "talk about anxiety." Many patients become psychiatry-wise, and by using the appropriate emotional jargon can generate concern from relatives, friends, and physicians. This sympathetic concern frequently serves as "secondary gain" (called social reinforcement by behavior therapists) for the individual and plays a major part in the maintenance of the alleged symptoms.

The first step in any behavioral program aimed at emotions is to identify the observable concomitants of the emotion. What precedes it, what is the setting in which it occurs, and how does the person concretely express the emotion? How does the environment, including other people, respond to the person who expresses emotion? We are especially interested in making reliable observations—preferably first-hand, but also through a thorough psychiatric history—on the relationship between the emotional behavior and the environmental response it generates.

Sigmund Freud was aware of the importance of the interpersonal consequences of behavior in maintaining symptoms. In "Fragment of an Analysis of a Case of Hysteria," he wrote:

> The motives for being ill often begin to be active in childhood. A little girl in her greed for love does not enjoy having to share the affection of her parents with her brothers and sisters, and she notices that the whole of their affection is lavished on her once more whenever she arouses their anxiety by falling ill. She has now discovered a means of enticing out of her parents love, and will make use of that means as soon as she has the necessary psychical material at her disposal for producing an illness.
>
> When such a child has grown up to be a woman she may find all the demands she used to make in her childhood countered owing to her marriage with an inconsiderate husband, who may subjugate her will, mercilessly exploit her capacity for work, and lavish neither his affection nor his money on her. In that case ill health will be her one weapon for maintaining her position. It will procure for her the care she longs for; it will force her husband to make pecuniary sacrifices for her and to show her consideration, as he would never have done were she well; it will compel him to treat her with solicitude if she recovers, for otherwise a relapse will occur. Her state of ill-health will have every appearance of being objective and involuntary—the very doctor who treats her will bear witness to the fact; and for that reason she will not need to feel any conscious self-reproaches at making such successful use of a means which she found effective in her years of childhood. [p. 55]*

* Reprinted with permission of Basic Books, New York, from Fragment of an Analysis of a Case of Hysteria in Vol. 3 of *The collected papers of Sigmund Freud.* Copyright © 1959 by Basic Books, Inc.

Emotional people are often labelled with colloquial and clinical epithets which derive from the values held by those using the epithets. In their usage, however, the terms "hysterical," "primitive," "infantile," "nasty," "sadistic," and "crock" tell us very little about the actual behavior of the individual. They do tell us more about the circumstances or consequences of his behavior. Behavior, by itself, is neutral and value-free. Behavior is not "nasty" or "primitive," but produces nasty consequences or occurs in settings in which it is socially inappropriate or primitive.

If a patient complains of difficulty in expressing hostility when it is appropriate to do so, we must identify the characteristics of the situations in which he is having difficulty. We must also identify the exact kinds of behavior that denote "hostility," and should be learned in the therapeutic program. Of the two statements below, which one *behaviorally* identifies the patient's problem with the affect, hostility?

Mr. Smith is afraid of his own aggressive impulses and doesn't seem able to express appropriate anger . . . . turn to page 31.

Mr. Smith can assert himself on the job with his co-workers but becomes passively sullen when frustrated by his wife at home . . . . turn to page 29.

You have correctly chosen the statement that denotes the what, where, and when of Mr. Smith's problem. You are beginning to make an accurate behavioral analysis of the problem. Of course we need more discrete information such as *how* he asserts himself on the job (What kinds of assertive expressions are in his repertoire?), how does his wife frustrate him (What is the setting in which his problem appears?), and what happens when he sulks passively (What are the consequences of his behavior? Does he get his way then?).

In assessing emotional behavior we want to know specifically (1) what undesirable behavior is being manifested, (2) what the desired responses are like, (3) the setting in which the problem occurs and (4) the consequences of the maladaptive behavior.

You said that "Mr. Smith is afraid of his aggressive impulses and doesn't seem able to express appropriate anger." This statement is an interesting inference but in no way identifies the situations in which Mr. Smith functions inappropriately. We are not provided with data that would permit any such conclusion as, "Mr. Smith is afraid of his aggressive impulses," and therefore, have no right to the assumption that his fear is responsible for his lack of assertiveness. We are on soft ground in ascribing motives to Mr. Smith's behavior while we have not carefully and reliably described his behavioral deficit.

Remembering how we define behavior, go back to page 27 an pick the other answer.

The concept of symptom substitution is cherished by therapists working within the medical model of psychotherapy. They believe that removing a symptom will be fruitless—the "underlying conflict" will generate another one in its place just as an underlying site of infection will continue to produce symptoms even after the fever is reduced by aspirin. There is evidence that symptom substitution rarely occurs when psychiatric symptoms are alleviated (Ullmann & Krasner, 1965; Wolpe & Lazarus, 1966).

We must clarify the concept of symptom substitution. Relapses can occur when an individual is re-exposed to the symptom-producing situation. New problems can arise if he encounters new pathogenic situations. Secondary gain is usually in play when new problem behaviors replace old ones. Interest, concern, solicitude and sympathy offered by friends, relatives, or even a therapist can help to maintain and perpetuate a long-term problem. When problem behavior that has gained attention from others is removed by treatment, the patient will seek to maintain the attention by other means. If more adaptive behavior is not within his repertoire, or if others in his life cannot be taught to respond contingently to "healthy" behavior, then atavistic or immature behavior, latent since childhood, will emerge and generally succeed in engaging the desired attention and recognition.

A brief case example will suffice to document this point. An adolescent boy was tyrannizing his parents with inappropriate demands for material nurturance. The family therapist helped the parents to set limits with their son. As they stopped complying with him, his demands decreased. Soon, however, he made a suicide gesture. An analysis of the situation revealed that although the therapist had helped the parents say "No" to the boy's demands, he did not simultaneously encourage them to say "Yes" to signs of more mature behavior which the boy had begun to demonstrate.

The lesson is clear: Always strive to replace maladaptive behavior with positive behavior rather than leaving this process to chance.

One way of organizing the presenting problem behaviorally is to see whether the problem involves primarily a *surplus* of maladaptive behavior (for example, the compulsive who checks the door locks a dozen times before going to sleep), or a *deficit* of adaptive behavior (for example, the autistic child who lacks speech). Organizing the problem in this manner helps to focus on the goals of treatment. Should we formulate a treatment program which builds up new behavior (for deficit problems) or which removes or decreases current, surplus behavior? Most of the time we try to construct a therapeutic program which does both. It is most efficacious to work out a *replacement* of symptoms with desirable behavior rather than to effect only the removal of symptoms.

The homosexual patient will have to learn how to "make it" socially with women if a treatment program aimed at removing his homosexual preferences is to succeed. The child who is excessively attached to adults will have to be taught to interact with other children as well as to expect less from adults. The patient "cured" of his stuttering by behavioral techniques may have to learn how to cope with many social situations that he previously avoided. Once the target behaviors for removal and replacement have been chosen, the appropriate behavioral techniques can be implemented.

Defining the deficits and surpluses in the patient is a preliminary to the construction of a behavioral analysis and a prescription for change.

Mr. Ballou has been continuously hospitalized for fifteen years. He is mute and socially withdrawn and spends hours on end pacing the corridors of the ward. During meetings he ignores questions or remarks made to him and turns away from the rest of the group. One of his symptoms is hoarding burned-out matches which he accumulates in his clothing and bed.

Are all of the following statements accurate behavioral descriptions of Mr. Ballou's problems?

A. Hoarding old matches is maladaptive surplus behavior.
B. Failure to respond to others in a group represents a deficit in his behavior.
C. Pacing is maladaptive surplus behavior.
D. Lack of speech is a deficit in his behavioral repertoire.

No.. turn to page 37.

Yes... turn to page 39.

Since the statements are all accurate, perhaps I can clarify by saying that a behavioral description rests on the exact specification of overt actions. Each of the statements on the list are easily verifiable acts. Several different observers of Mr. Ballou's behavior could agree on identifying his surpluses and deficits. Little or no inference is required. If we were to go a step further in a behavioral analysis, we might want to know more about the frequency of Mr. Ballou's pacing or the circumstances surrounding his hoarding of matches, particularly the response it evokes in the nurses and attendants. For the time being we will hold off on taking this additional step.

Re-read page 35 and then pick the correct answer.

You correctly said that all the statements on the list are accurate descriptions of Mr. Ballou's problem. Having identified the problems in specific behavioral terms, you are now ready to determine their functional causes and then work out a behavior therapy. The next section of the book will take you through these additional steps.

By this time you must be wondering how behavior therapists avoid the ethical pitfall of arbitrarily defining problems and solutions. In actual practice, the pitfall is more apparent than real since the patient has usually defined his problem by the time he has come for help. The behavior therapist then simply collaborates with the patient to put the complaint in behavioral terms. Extended evaluations can be useful in assisting a patient or family to clarify their distress, problems and ambivalences prior to setting goals for treatment. At other times a patient is not in a position to collaborate actively with the therapist in defining the problem as in the case of a chronically hospitalized, regressed, psychotic patient or an autistic child. Here, the behavioral excesses and deficits are so grossly discrepant from commonly held standards of normality that the statement of goals and problems can be accepted by most people. In any event, the behavioral approach to psychiatry and counseling does place the therapist in a position of responsibility for deciding upon standards of normality–abnormality, adaptation–maladaptation, and maturity–immaturity. We would hope that the clinician, by virtue of his professional training and humanitarian principles, is a person qualified to make these assessments.

Now it is clear that the first step in behavior therapy—defining the problems and the therapeutic goals—is very much like aspects of short-term, goal-oriented, sector, and ego-supportive therapies. All these techniques have in common their orientation toward specific and approachable goals and a constant focus on where the patient is and where he is headed. The therapist can from the start see the goals and work with the patient toward achieving them.

SUMMARY OF CHAPTER 1

1. The first step in behavior therapy is to identify the patient's problem(s) in specific, concrete, observable terms. This is the process of describing behavior.

2. Language and thoughts reported by the patient are verbal behavior and are relevant domains for the behavior therapist.

3. Affects can be dealt with in behavior therapy as long as they can be clearly and reliably described by the patient or observed in their behavioral forms by the therapist.

4. One convenient means of organizing a patient's problem in behavioral terms is to decide which behaviors are excessive (undesirable, maladaptive) and which are lacking (desirable, adaptive). This helps the therapist and patient to define the therapeutic goals.

5. Identifying the problem is a joint, collaborative endeavor between the patient and the therapist; however, when a severely disturbed or regressed patient cannot cooperate in this effort, commonly accepted and shared values are used to define the clinical problems and the therapeutic goals.

Chapter 2: THE ENVIRONMENTAL DETERMINANTS OF BEHAVIOR

In the first chapter we have shown how to initiate a behavioral analysis of a psychiatric problem. Identifying the problem as a set of observable actions must be done before proceeding further. In this section, we will describe how events in the environment generate and maintain problem behaviors. We will also discuss some of the methods that have developed from experimental psychology which form the basis for clinical behavior modification.

All behavior occurs in an environmental context with stimuli and events preceding and following it. The regularity of the interaction between environment and behavior, assessed by careful observation and measurement, allows us to build a science of behavior. Stimulation of the patellar tendon produces a knee jerk. Placing meat in front of a food-deprived dog produces salivation. A loud noise will make a baby cry. These are unconditioned responses to unconditioned stimuli, and can also be elicited by neutral or conditioned stimuli paired with the unconditioned stimuli. Examples of conditioned stimuli which can elicit responses are:

    a. The ringing of a bell (conditioned stimulus) which can produce salivation (response) in a dog after it is paired with food (unconditioned stimulus) for several days.

    b. A rabbit (conditioned stimulus) which can cause a baby to cry (response) after it is repeatedly presented to the baby at the same time as a loud noise (unconditioned stimulus).

Behavior can also be determined by the stimuli or occurrences which regularly follow it in time. Salaries are the consequences that maintain work behavior. For many people, grades serve as powerful consequences that support studying. Orgasms are the consequences that maintain sexual behavior. The occasional jackpot maintains efforts and expenditures with a slot machine. Because we associate these positive consequences to the relevant past behavior, we learn to exhibit the same behavior in anticipation of again receiving the desired consequences.

We can see that careful observation enables us to be sensitive to the interplay between behavior and the events that precede or follow it. To be able to know when behavior is changing under environmental influence, we have to measure or record behavior. We can measure intensity of behavior, but a more reliable and convenient way is to measure its frequency.

Clinically, we want to know what environmental conditions, especially in the interpersonal environment, are maintaining the patient's maladaptive behavior or preventing adaptive behavior from emerging. While it is of interest to have knowledge of the conditions which led to the problem behavior or syndrome (the conditioning or developmental history), our major focus will be on the *current*, functional relations between the individual and his environment.

The factors that led to acquisition of a problem behavior are important for the immediate purposes of therapy only insofar as they currently operate to maintain the behavior or to prevent the learning of new, desired behaviors.

When we record changes in the frequency of some selected behavior as well as associated changes in the environment we discover the lawfulness of human behavior. If the frequency of Johnny's temper tantrums decreases when his mother ignores them but increases when she reacts to them, we can make an empirical statement about what is motivating the tantrums.

Recording the frequency of behavior provides a means of following the progress of problem behavior, and new adaptive behavior which is developed in the course of therapy. Such a record helps the therapist to judge the effectiveness of a treatment procedure. Since behavior therapy is an empirical technology, evaluation success and failure is part of the process of developing new and effective methods.

Let us take an example of clinical behavior and see if we can measure the functional relationship between the problem and the environment.

Mrs. Lane, a 37-year-old woman who has been depressed since the death of her mother, is observed in her home by her therapist. The therapist records each instance of "depressive-like" behavior, such as crying, complaining about somatic symptoms, pacing, and withdrawal. He also notes the consequences of these behaviors. Initially, Mrs. Lane has a high rate of these depressive behaviors (*see* Fig. 1) and it is noted that members of the family frequently respond to these with sympathy, concern, and helpfulness. During this time, her rate of adaptive actions as a housewife and mother are very low, but she does make occasional efforts to cook, clean house, and attend to the children's needs.

The therapist, in family sessions, instructs the husband and children to pay instant and frequent attention to Mrs. Lane's coping behavior and to gradually ignore her depressed behavior. They were taught to acknowledge her positive actions with interest, encouragement, and approval. Overall, they were not to decrease the amount of attention focused on Mrs. Lane but rather switch the contingencies of their attention from "sick woman" to "housewife and mother." Within one week, Mrs. Lane's depressed behavior decreased sharply and her "healthy" behavior increased.

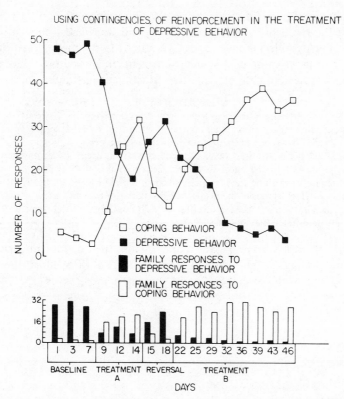

USING CONTINGENCIES OF REINFORCEMENT IN THE TREATMENT OF DEPRESSIVE BEHAVIOR

NUMBER OF RESPONSES

□ COPING BEHAVIOR
■ DEPRESSIVE BEHAVIOR
■ FAMILY RESPONSES TO DEPRESSIVE BEHAVIOR
□ FAMILY RESPONSES TO COPING BEHAVIOR

BASELINE   TREATMENT   REVERSAL   TREATMENT
               A   B
DAYS

Fig. 1. Modification of depressive behavior using reinforcement techniques taught to family members. (From Liberman, R. P., & Raskin, D. E. Depression: A Behavioral Formulation. *Archives of General Psychiatry*, 1971, **24**, 515–523.)

The record of Mrs. Lane's behavior made by the therapist is presented in Fig. 1 together with the amount of responses by family members given to depressed behavior (dark bar) and to coping behavior (light bar).

In this example, the precipitating event was probably Mrs. Lane's loss of her mother. The graph portrays the consequences of her problem behavior. Choose the correct answer:

Mrs. Lane's depressive behavior and her coping behavior are both maintained and supported by the consequences they engender in her interpersonal milieu; namely, the attentive responses of her family members........turn to page 49.

Mrs. Lane's depression, precipitated by the loss of her mother, got better only because of the passage of time since all depressions sooner or later spontaneously remit .... turn to page 51.

The behavioral point of view stresses the importance of (1) observing and recording the frequencies of specific verbal and non-verbal behavior in an objective and reliable manner; and (2) noting the functional relationships between the behavior and its associated environmental events. Skinner (1953) has stated this viewpoint in reference to a scientific understanding of emotion:

> As long as we conceive of the problem of emotion as one of inner states, we are not likely to advance a practical technology (for remedying dysphoric states). It does not help in the solution of a practical problem to be told that some feature of a man's behavior is due to frustration or anxiety (or depression); we also need to be told how the frustration, anxiety (or depression) has been induced and how it may be altered. In the end, we find ourselves dealing with two events—the emotional behavior and the manipulable conditions of which that behavior is a function—which comprise the proper subject matter of the study of emotion . . . the objection to inner states is not that they do not exist, but that they are not relevant to a functional analysis.*

Behavior therapists have begun to analyze and treat depressions using the functional approach suggested by Skinner. Reviews of these efforts have been written by Lewinsohn *et al.* (1969) and Liberman and Raskin (1971).

---

* Reprinted with permission of The Macmillan Company, New York, from B. F. Skinner's *Science and human behavior.* Copyright © 1953 by Macmillan.

You are accurately pinpointing the functional tie-up between environment and behavior. Mrs. Lane's difficulties, while elicited by the loss of her mother, were indeed maintained by the consequences they produced in those close to her. The causal association between her depression and its interpersonal consequences was demonstrated by a brief clinical experiment. After the 14th day of observation, the therapist instructed the family members to return to providing Mrs. Lane with attention and solicitude for her complaints. Within three days, Mrs. Lane was once again showing a high level of depressive behavior, albeit not as high as initially. When the focus of the family members' attentiveness was finally moved back to her coping ability and away from her miserableness, Mrs. Lane quickly improved. One year after termination, Mrs. Lane was continuing to function well without feeling depressed.

While good behavior therapy or analysis does not always require rigorous charting and graphing of behavior, some approximation to this ideal is necessary for effective treatment. At the minimum, a therapist must keep clearly in mind the progress made by the patient in moving from the problem behaviors to the therapeutic goals.

Turn to page 53.

It is true that depressions tend to remit over a period of time, but whether this occurs "spontaneously" or not is open to serious question. Many changes can occur in the environment of a depressed person which, over time, can produce symptomatic improvement. Thus, if a depressed individual begins to obtain recognition from others for attempting to return to functioning normally and gradually loses the concern and sympathy from impatient and fed-up relatives, his behavior would be expected to improve.

In the case of Mrs. Lane, a clinical experiment was performed to prove the causal link between her behavior and the responses generated in her family. After the 14th day, the therapist instructed the family members to return to providing Mrs. Lane with attention and solicitude for her complaints. Within three days, Mrs. Lane was once again showing a high level of depressive behavior, albeit not as high as initially. When the focus of the family members' attentiveness was finally moved back to her coping ability and away from her miserableness, Mrs. Lane quickly improved. One year after termination, Mrs. Lane was continuing to function well without depressive symptoms.

Turn to the last paragraph on page 49.

A positive reinforcer is defined, not by its intrinsic quality or characteristics, but by the effect it has on behavior. Any presenting consequence of behavior which increases the probability of the behavior's occurrence is defined as a positive reinforcer. Events may follow behavior which appear to be noxious or negative in quality, but they may actually serve as positive reinforcers. Spankings and scoldings, aversive on the surface, may on closer scrutiny have the effect of increasing the frequency of the "naughty" behavior. This is particularly the case in families where there is an overall lack of attention given the children. The state of social deprivation apparently sensitizes the child to any form of attention provided by the parents.

The clinical problem of masochism is another example of apparently aversive stimuli actually positively reinforcing certain behaviors. We must realize that the physical attributes of a stimulus do not determine whether that stimulus is pleasant or aversive. Stimuli which produce approach reactions in an individual may be labelled as pleasant. Conversely, a physical event such as a spanking, flagellation, or a loud noise can be defined as aversive if it leads to escape or avoidance reactions by a given individual. The aversiveness or pleasantness of a particular stimulus must be defined in terms of the resulting behavior in a given individual under specific circumstances. Cigarette smoke could be viewed as pleasant for a long-term smoker but noxious for a person inhaling for the first time. When we say that a person is behaving masochistically, we are saying that he is approaching a stimulus which most individuals in our society reject or avoid. The stimulus might even be one that the "masochist" would avoid under different conditions or if other choices were open to him.

The masochist enjoys and goes to great lengths to obtain beatings or other forms of personal degradation. While submitting to beatings would be aversive and revolting to most people, masochists have associated this stimulus with pleasure (e.g., sexual excitement) sometime during their past histories. The pain becomes a conditioned reinforcer and can motivate a whole range of complex behaviors.

SUMMARY OF CHAPTER 2

1. The regularity of the interaction between an individual's behavior (past and current) and its environmental context provides the necessary starting point for a science of behavior.

2. By recording the frequency of some selected behavior together with associated changes in the environment, we discover the lawfulness of human behavior.

3. The behavioral clinician's emphasis is on (a) objectively observing and counting the frequency of behavior, and (b) noting the functional relationships between the behavior and its temporally related environmental events.

4. In making a behavioral analysis, we want to know what environmental conditions—particularly the interpersonal or human environment—are maintaining the problem behavior or preventing more adaptive behavior from emerging.

Chapter 3: REINFORCEMENT: POSITIVE AND NEGATIVE

Operant conditioning refers to the process by which behavior is changed as a result of consequences generated in the environment. Operant behavior is behavior of any person that literally *operates* on the environment to produce effects. The effects produced in the environment, in turn, can determine the rate or intensity of the behavior. For instance, the child who receives his teacher's attention when he is noisy and restless, but is ignored when he is acting "good," will continue or even increase his noisiness and restlessness.

Consequences of behavior that serve to increase the frequency or intensity of the behavior are called reinforcers. Consonant with its common-sense definition, a reinforcer builds up or strengthens behavior on which it is contingent. Reinforcers can be positive or negative.

Positive reinforcers strengthen behavior on which they focus or are contingent time-wise. The pupil noted above was positively reinforced by his teacher's attentiveness for being noisy. A weekly wage positively reinforces attendance at a job since payment is contingent upon time spent at work. In a mental hospital setting, tender-loving-care can actually reinforce the very behavior which the staff wishes to terminate; for example, repeated suicide gestures are largely motivated by the concern and protectiveness generated in the staff members.

Mrs. Fraidy was depressed and apathetic when she came to the Day Hospital. She had given up her active interest in golfing, sewing and antiques, and was afraid to drive her car. In Southern California, not driving means severe restrictions on one's opportunities in engaging in social and recreational activities.

A plan was formulated which was aimed at reinforcing her driving efforts. The nurse who was her therapist got Mrs. Fraidy to bring in a local street map. Each day Mrs. Fraidy was to drive her car over a new route and then return to the Day Hospital and plot her journey on the map in red ink. The nurse responded to Mrs. Fraidy's small excursions around the County with interest, questions about the drive, and approval. Whenever Mrs. Fraidy failed to make a drive or repeated an old route, her nurse ignored her.

Within two weeks Mrs. Fraidy was driving all over the County and began to recapture her previous interests and hobbies.

Behavior which is *strengthened or increased* by the *escape from or avoidance* of a particular consequence is maintained by negative reinforcement. We keep our distance from meddling relatives and hot stove burners. Both are negative reinforcers because they have consequences which maintain "keep away" behavior. A person who is "afraid" to fly in airplanes shows a variety of behavior in travelling which is maintained by the avoidance of the fear associated with planes. Such a person might undergo hardship and duress travelling on trains or driving the car long distances in order to avoid air travel. Phobias in general are maintained by the process of negative reinforcement. So long as the individual avoids the phobic object or situation, he can avoid the anticipated anxiety. Constructing therapeutic programs which make it possible for the individual to successfully reality-test irrational fears has been a major accomplishment of behavior therapists. We will become familar with some of these programs as we proceed through the book.

In summary, positive and negative reinforcers are consequences of behavior which serve to strengthen the behavior that precedes them. In the case of positive reinforcement, the behavior produces the appearance of the reinforcer while in negative reinforcement the behavior avoids or moves away from the reinforcer.

Negative reinforcement has been used by behavior therapists to induce adaptive behavior change. For instance, one investigator introduced a loud, noxious noise through a loudspeaker hidden in a vent whenever a therapy group of schizophrenics fell silent for more than one minute. As soon as a patient broke the silence, the noise was turned off. Within several sessions, the group was converted from a slow-moving silent one to a lively, talkative one (Heckel *et al.*, 1962).

Sexual deviations have been treated by a type of negative reinforcement procedure called avoidance conditioning. Working with homosexuals who wished to change their sexual pattern, one experimenter (Birk, 1969) projected at random erotic pictures of men and women onto a screen. By pressing a button, the patient could change the picture on the screen. Small but painful electric shocks were unpredictably delivered to the patient's forearm when the male pictures were viewed for more than one second. Pressing the button and moving a female picture into view led to avoidance or escape from the shock, depending on how quickly the button was pressed. Some investigators have used a penile plethysmograph—a device which measures the volume of the penis and hence the amount of erection—instead of "viewing behavior" as the relevant response on which to base shock. The results of these studies have shown significant changes in sexual behavior particularly when other supportive measures, such as group therapy with male and female co-therapists, have been used.

Describe some situations which embody negative reinforcement. Draw upon day-to-day behaviors as well as clinical ones. Turn to page 61 after describing at least five situations and see if you have added new ones to the author's list.

Here are additional examples of negative reinforcement in operation. Can you add new ones to the list?

> The person who cheats on an exam to avoid getting a low mark.
>
> The construction of dikes and dams to avoid floods.
>
> Paying premiums on disability insurance to avoid impoverishment when ill.
>
> Putting on sunglasses to escape from the glare of the sun.
>
> Turning up the thermostat to escape from cold.
>
> Buying and using an air conditioner to escape from or avoid the heat.
>
> The hit-and-run driver who leaves his victim out of fear of legal sanctions.
>
> Hospitalizing a suicidal patient to prevent self-destruction.
>
> Using insulin to avoid hyperglycemia and diabetic complications.
>
> Using maintenance doses of phenothiazines or anti-depressants to avoid relapses.
>
> Obeying traffic signals to avoid legal punishment.
>
> Almost all behaviors governed by laws are motivated by negative reinforcement, the avoidance of fines or prison.
>
> The frigid woman who avoids sexual intercourse because it is unpleasant.
>
> We used to put calamine lotion on our insect bites to *escape* from the pain and itching, but now we use insect repellants to *avoid* the bites altogether.

Family therapy was being conducted with an 18-year-old boy, who had been addicted to narcotics, and his parents. An impasse was reached during summer vacation with the boy spending all his time at home watching television. The boy indicated that he wanted to get a job, but did not feel he had the "energy." His parents wanted him to be working, but had given up nagging him about it. The therapist suggested the following "contract." The boy would have continued access to his television set, but only by paying $1.00 per hour for its use. Unless the rental fee was paid, the parents would keep the TV set in their possession. Since the boy had no savings and since he had a history of successful job experience, he was soon working and watching TV.

A 24-year-old married woman had completed desensitization therapy (*see* Chapter 9) for frigidity but could not wilfully try out her progress in sexual practice with her husband. Her therapist took an inventory of the activities she engaged in regularly before going to bed. She indicated that she couldn't go to sleep without brushing her teeth. An agreement was made whereby she would brush her teeth at night only contingent upon her first engaging in sexual activity with her husband. Her teeth went unbrushed for two nights and then she had successful sexual intercourse, with orgasm, for the first time in her life. A six month follow-up revealed both clean teeth and an active, satisfying sexual life.

One very clinically useful principle of positive reinforcement is called the Premack Principle, after the psychologist who first enunciated it (Premack, 1959). One can phrase the principle in this manner: Any behavior which has a high frequency of occurrence can be used in a contingent fashion to reinforce a different behavior which has a low frequency of occurrence. A patient who daily goes out on the hospital grounds to feed birds and squirrels but who rarely attends group therapy sessions can be motivated to increase his group therapy attendance by permitting him access to the grounds *contingent* upon his going to group therapy. If a patient who does not carry out her work assignments is observed to frequently converse with a nurse, her work performance can be increased by making contact with the nurse contingent upon fulfilling her assignments.

The application of the Premack Principle enables the clinician to select reinforcers which are appropriate for each individual. Not all patients will be motivated by candy, cigarettes, or opportunity to watch TV. Some patients may respond to other reinforcers, such as opportunity to mix with the opposite sex, visits to amusements outside the hospital, cosmetics, a chance to be first in line for meals, or even talks with a chaplain or psychiatrist. What is reinforcing for each person must be determined empirically and one convenient way to make this determination is to observe what activities the patient preferentially engages in. Then these preferences can be used contingently to build up less frequent behavior which will be of benefit to the patient.

Reinforcers can be categorized according to their type and source. There are reinforcers like food and sex (positive) and pain (negative) which are termed *primary reinforcers* because of their physical and innate attributes. Money, possessions, honors, and attention from people—sometimes called secondary reinforcers—are of equal or even greater importance in generating and maintaining behavior among humans. In fact, with humans the so-called secondary reinforcers play the most important part in motivating behavior, especially behavior that has clinical relevance. That man's rewards come via language from other people distinguish him as a truly social animal.

Social reinforcement is a term used to describe the "goodies" that people dole out to one another such as approval, affection, attention, concern, interest, solicitude and sympathy. Experiments in verbal conditioning have shown that even a nod or a smile or a Mm-mm from the interviewer can significantly increase the frequency of almost any kind of verbal response in an interviewee—responses such as positive self-references, remarks about parents, feeling statements, childhood recollections, and cohesive remarks in a group. These findings have clear implications for the conduct of psychotherapy, and will be discussed further in Chapter 11.

Many behavioral problems embody a combination of positive and negative reinforcement. For example, the drug addict or alcoholic achieve a pleasurable state (i.e., feeling "high") and escape from distressing social anxiety by maintaining their habits. Their use of alcohol or drugs also are positively reinforced by the conviviality and cohesiveness of their fellow addicts (and sometimes the sympathy and nurturance of relatives) while being negatively reinforced by avoiding noxious withdrawal symptoms.

Another example of positive and negative reinforcement operating in a mother–child relationship to perpetuate a problem is given by Patterson and Reid (1967). Reciprocal reinforcement can maintain deviant behavior in a child who demands an ice cream cone while shopping with his mother in a supermarket. Typically, the reinforcer for this "demandingness" is compliance by the mother, but if she ignores the demand, the effect is to increase the rate or loudness of the demand. Loud demands or shrieks by a child in a supermarket are aversive to the mother; that is, her non-compliance is punished. When the mother finally buys the ice cream cone, the aversive tantrum ends. The positive reinforcer for the child's tantrum is the ice cream cone. The negative reinforcing contingency for the mother was the termination of the "scene" in the supermarket. In this reciprocal fashion, the tantrum behavior is perpetuated.

SUMMARY OF CHAPTER 3

1. *Positive* and *negative reinforcers* are consequences of behavior which serve to strengthen the behavior that generates them.

2. In positive reinforcement, the behavior produces the *appearance* or *onset* of the reinforcer and is subsequently increased in frequency as a result of this contingency.

3. In negative reinforcement, the behavior enables the individual to *avoid* or *move away* from the reinforcer. As a result of this contingency, the future likelihood of avoidance or escape behavior is increased.

4. Positive and negative reinforcement techniques are useful for *increasing* the rate of adaptive behavior.

5. Positive reinforcers are loosely called "rewards" and are often experienced as pleasant. Negative reinforcers are often viewed and felt as aversive or noxious. However, it is important to remember that a reinforcer is *not* defined by its intrinsic properties, by subjective feelings, or by cultural stereotypes. Rather, a stimulus becomes a reinforcer when it *actually results in changes in the frequency of behavior*. Stimuli or events that increase the behavior they are contingent upon are positive reinforcers. Stimuli or events that increase behavior which avoids or escapes from them are negative reinforcers. Sometimes, stimuli which seem aversive or painful may actually be positive reinforcers; conversely, seemingly pleasant or enjoyable stimuli or events may actually be negative reinforcers. A reinforcer is defined by the effect it has on behavior.

Chapter 4: SHAPING BEHAVIOR BY SUCCESSIVE APPROXIMATIONS

Perhaps the most important behavioral principle for clinical application is that of *shaping* behavior. Shaping involves working gradually toward a specified goal by reinforcing successive steps toward the goal. This method, also called conditioning by successive approximation, is used to develop desirable behavior that is not already in the patient's repertoire. The therapist shapes the available behaviors into the desired end product, capitalizing on the variability and regularity of successive behaviors. The shaping process involves the reinforcement of selected responses which proceed in the desired direction and the non-reinforcement of those which do not.

If you are trying to reinstate speech in a chronic schizophrenic patient who has been mute for 20 years, for example, you can't afford to wait for him to utter some words before issuing reinforcement. He may never say a word spontaneously and you will be caught holding the reward. Instead you must reward him for the slightest approximation toward speech, such as silent movements of his lips or a grunt. You may make sounds yourself for him to imitate and then reinforce his approximating your modeling.

When shaping behavior you must remember to:

1. Begin where the patient is at.
2. Don't expect too much progress at once.
3. Move at the patient's pace.
4. Offer reinforcement for stepwise approximations to the final desired, behavioral goal.

Shaping is thus particularly useful in situations where the desired response rarely if ever occurs, or if the therapist does not wish to wait for it to occur.

Talented therapists use the principle of shaping almost intuitively as the description of the following interaction indicates (Ferster & Simons, 1966).

Jackie was reluctant to leave the room one day after his therapist had been swinging and tumbling with him. Instead of continuing to play with him or sending him away, she held him in front of a puzzle, put one piece in his hand and held his hand over the appropriate place until he dropped it. The puzzle was of the simplest form, so a slight nudge on his part jarred it into place. When he fit the puzzle into its exact place his therapist reacted instantly and enthusiastically. She led him to an open area where she roughhoused with him, but only for about a minute. They then went back to the puzzle where this time he not only dropped it into the right place, but he nudged it into position without his therapist guiding his hand during the final maneuver. She approved immediately, as before, and played with him again for another minute. In each of perhaps 10 such successive experiences (about 15 min), she required a little more of the boy each time until finally he picked up a piece, put it into place, walked to where she had been taking him for play and lay on the floor with his hands up, wanting her to play with him. On successive days the roughhousing activity was contingent on more sustained and complicated performance with the puzzles. Finally, Jackie assembled three or four different puzzles, some much more difficult than the first one, before being reinforced.

The puzzle itself is an example of a natural reinforcer. The difficulty of the puzzle specifies a schedule of intermittent reinforcement. Its physical design determines much of the behavior appropriate to completing it. In a very simple puzzle, almost any performance gets the piece in place and hence reinforcement is virtually continuous; but as the pieces become even slightly irregular, the child may need to make several attempts, only one of which will be reinforced. With more difficult puzzles, there are more possibilities on nonreinforced responses, and a graded series of puzzles is a convenient device for changing from continuous to intermittent reinforcement. Eventually the reinforcement again becomes continuous when the person becomes skilled. Laboratory experience has shown that such a graded experience from continuous to intermittent reinforcement is the best way to develop a persistent, durable repertoire.

The small amount of restraint the therapist imposed on Jackie during his first encounter with the puzzle insured that other behavior, incompatible with puzzle-solving, would not interfere in the shaping. The actual reinforcer maintaining the puzzle activity was his therapist's immediate verbal response, which in turn derived from the roughhousing. Eventually the therapist shifted the control to the puzzle itself, which later came to be the only event preceding the roughhousing.*

In this example, Jackie's ability to solve puzzles was developed or shaped in a gradual, stepwise fashion. Each successful approximation to the goal was rewarded by his therapist.

---

* Reprinted with permission of the authors and the Psychological Record, from C. B. Ferster and Jeanne Simons' Behavior Therapy with Children in the *Psychological Record*, Vol. 16, pp. 65–71, 1966. Copyright © 1966 by the Psychological Record.

Let us try our hand with shaping a specific case example.

Mona is a four-year-old girl who attends a therapeutic nursery school for emotionally disturbed children. One of her major difficulties is a complete lack of social play with peers. She clings to adults and withdraws from any involvement with other children. When forcibly placed in a sandbox or on a jungle gym near other kids, she screams and runs toward the nearest adult. Mona has a good relationship with the nursery school teacher and the latter, instructed in the use of behavioral methods, decides to use her relationship selectively as a reinforcer for shaping Mona's behavior toward cooperative play with other students. The teacher first plans a program which she will follow in reinforcing Mona, using attention and approval as the reinforcer.

The program with the best chance to succeed is stepwise reinforcement of Mona:

> Looking at other children (step 1)
> Walking a few paces toward other children (step 2)
> Turning toward a child who invites her to join a game (step 3)
> Standing near children involved in a game (step 4)
> Playing alone in the sandbox or on the jungle gym in parallel with other children who are separately playing (step 5)
> Spending increasing amounts of time observing children in play (steps 7–10)
> Making tentative moves toward engaging in activity with children (step 11)
> Playing a simple game with another child who invites her participation (step 12)
> Initiating play with another child (step 13)
> Spontaneously entering into group games (step 14) .... turn to page 73.
> Taking several steps toward other children (step 1)
> Talking with other children (step 2)
> Playing a game with one other child (step 3)
> Spontaneously entering into group games (step 4) ....turn to page 75.

A frequent problem found in state hospitals is the inaudible speech of long-term patients. Institutionalization leads to the weakening of many behaviors which a person possesses when he enters the mental hospital. In large hospitals, silence and compliance is reinforced by an overburdened nursing staff and therefore many patients learn to "mumble".

Three "mumblers" in a state hospital were taught to increase the loudness of their speech by a shaping procedure. The patients stood at a set distance from a microphone which was connected to a voice-activated relay. The relay, an electronic device sensitive to noise, would close, flashing a light signal, when the patient's vocal intensity exceeded a predetermined level. The patient received candy and cigarette reinforcement when his voice activated the relay and produced a light flash.

Initially, the relay was pre-set at a very low threshold level so that even a mumbled phrase would produce a light flash. Gradually and in a stepwise fashion, the threshold for the relay was increased as each patient learned to raise his voice. Louder and louder speech was required during daily trials in order to gain reinforcement. Within two months, the patients were talking at normal tones of voice. The improvement was carried over to the ward setting by having the nurses respond to the patients only when they spoke audibly.

You are sensitive to the importance of breaking down the approximations to the desired behavior into small, discrete steps. The steps must be small to increase the likelihood of success and they must be discrete and observable so that the teacher will be able to immediately recognize the time for reinforcement. Developing a program ahead of time is necessary since the teacher (or therapist, or parent) must anticipate the desired response in order to reinforce it *immediately*. Delayed reinforcement will not work as well since other, undesired behaviors may intervene and be inadvertently reinforced.

Skillful shaping is somewhat of an art that requires experience as well as knowledge of technique. The therapist must select the appropriate response for reinforcement and must know how long to reinforce any one response before moving on to the next one. If the therapist continues to reinforce an approximation for too long, the patient may become satiated with the reinforcer or the approximation may become so firmly stabilized that it will be difficult to move the patient along to the next step. On the other hand, if the therapist moves too rapidly from one step to another, the behavior already shaped may extinguish and it will become necessary to backtrack to an earlier level and start over again. If too great a step is required of the patient, the frustration from not receiving expected reinforcement can lead to emotional behavior (for instance, a temper tantrum) that will disrupt the entire learning effort.

To review another clinical example of shaping, turn to page 75.

If you used this program with Mona you might wait a very long time before she emits even the first step. In fact, you might have to wait so long that the school session would be over first.

In constructing a program for shaping behavior, you should keep in mind that each step must have a good likelihood of occurring. Expecting too much too soon will not lead anywhere. While it is likely that Mona might occasionally glance at other children at play, it is far less likely—knowing her past behavior—that she will spontaneously take some steps toward other children.

Here is an example of a program that succeeded in shaping a somewhat different behavior in a mentally-retarded child—the putting on of a coat, using candy as a reinforcer.

> Coat put on child by the therapist with one hand still in sleeve,
> Child reinforced for pushing hand the rest of the way through sleeve (step 1)
> One hand in armhole of coat,
> Child reinforced for pushing hand through entire sleeve (step 2)
> One hand in armhole and other hand still in sleeve,
> Child reinforced for pushing both hands through sleeves (step 3)
> Both hands in armholes of coat,
> Child reinforced for pushing both hands through sleeves (step 4)
> One hand in armhole of coat, other hand hanging free,
> Child reinforced for pushing both hands through sleeves (step 5)
> Both hands hanging free, coat over child's shoulders,
> Child reinforced for pushing arms through sleeves (step 6)

Note that in this case the shaping seems to move backwards; however, we are starting at the child's functional level—receiving assistance from an adult in putting on the coat—and progressing gradually toward greater self-help. Each step should be reinforced several times before you are assured it is within the child's repertoire and move on to the next step.

Turn to page 71, and choose the correct answer.

An ingenious use of the principle of shaping was made by Schwitzgebel (1966) who wanted to teach juvenile delinquents to put their feelings into words. En route to the final goal, which was to get the teenagers to express their emotions into a tape recorder, the investigator reinforced them for each step along the pathway. At first, he gave them money and cigarettes for meeting him at their streetcorner hangouts. Then he told them they could get money if they would take a trip with him on the subway. Next, they had to meet him at a particular subway station across town, if they were to receive their money. In successive steps they were reinforced for (1) coming to a storefront office used by Schwitzgebel, (2) saying anything into the tape recorder, and (3) speaking about experiences and relationships which were emotionally important to them. This shaping procedure led to a strong positive attachment between the delinquents—all of whom had arrest records —and the researchers. A two year follow-up indicated that the boys who were exposed to this "streetcorner research" had one-half the recidivism of boys in a matched control group.

An early report of the reinstatement of verbal behavior in mute schizophrenics that graphically describes the shaping process has been replicated many times. The author-therapists were psychology students working on a project for a seminar on operant conditioning. The following narrative describes the case of a catatonic patient, Mr. Allen, who sat immobile, imperturbable, and unresponsive to attempts to engage his attention by verbal means or by offerings of cigarettes. When a package of chewing gum accidentally fell out of the therapist's pocket, the latter noted that the patient's eyes followed the gum. Here, then, were a response and a reinforcer to use in the shaping procedure, which was carried out three times a week. During the first two weeks, the therapist held up some gum and waited for the patient's eyes to focus on it. Then he gave the patient the gum. At the end of two weeks, the patient's eyes moved toward the gum as soon as it was presented.

Next, the therapist reinforced Mr. Allen with gum for any movement of his mouth or lips. By the end of the third week, both lip and eye movements occurred when the gum was held up. Then the therapist withheld the gum until Mr. Allen made a vocalization, such as a grunt. By the end of the fourth week, lip, eye movements and vocalizations were in Mr. Allen's repertoire. During the fifth and sixth weeks, the therapist held up the gum and said, "Say gum, gum," and he reinforced imitative approximations to the word "gum." After the sixth week (18 sessions) the patient spontaneously said, "Gum, please" and then went on to answer questions about his name and age.

Thereafter, Mr. Allen responded to questions from his therapist both in individual and group sessions and on the ward, but remained mute and impassive to others. To generalize the speaking responses and to overcome the stimulus control of the therapist, other staff members were brought into the room with the therapist and the patient. The patient soon directed speech to others who responded to him only when he verbalized his questions and not when he grunted, grimaced, or used sign language. (Isaacs *et al.*, 1960).

In shaping Mr. Allen's verbalization the therapist reinforced successive approximations to speech such as:

Eye movement, mouth and lip movements, primitive vocalizations, words, and finally verbal requests and responses ....turn to page 81.

Facial movements, words, and finally verbal requests and responses........ ....turn to page 83.

Perhaps you noticed in the case study of Mr. Allen that the therapist used other techniques in addition to shaping. One was stimulus generalization which involved the association of other staff members in the reinforcement process. Reinforcement, initially associated with therapist's presence alone, now was given in the presence of others as well. In this manner speech spread or generalized to other people.

Another behavioral technique used was modeling or imitation which occurred when the therapist cued the patient by saying, "Say gum, gum." Prompting through the conscious use of the therapist's behavior as a model is an important principle which will be taken up in greater detail in Chapter 13.

You have seen also the phenomenon of response generalization which occurred when the patient began to use many words after having emitted the first few. When the response, "gum" was reinforced, other responses in the same class occurred without further reinforcement. Response generalization is found in all species—in man its utility in verbal behavior is apparent. It eliminated the necessity for the therapist to reinforce every word in order to increase Mr. Allen's vocabulary. The therapist concentrated on one word and in reinstating it, reinstated words in general. Additional examples of this generalization effect will be given in Chapter 13 which deals with behavior therapy of autistic children.

Right. You said the successive approximations were "eye movements, lip movements, vocalizations, words, and finally verbal requests and responses." You know that constituent responses making up the successive approximations to speech must be discrete and gradual in progression. It would be good practice for you to make up a desired end-response and then construct the hierarchy of successive approximations. Use a clinical problem you are familiar with.

Incorrect. Although your answer outlines the overall procedure, the essence of shaping is the identification of *discrete* responses each of which gradually approximates the desired end-response and is sequentially reinforced. If the therapist began his procedure by reinforcing the response class, "facial expressions," he might still be working with Mr. Allen today. The group of responses encompassed by "facial expressions" is too broad and does not give the therapist sufficient instruction. Should he reinforce eye blinks, grimaces, smiles, scowls?

Furthermore, the progression of responses, "facial expressions—words," leaves out the discrete interval, "primitive vocalizations" which are more likely to occur before a fully-formed work and hence should be a step in the sequence of approximations.

Return to page 79 and choose the other answer.

SUMMARY OF CHAPTER 4

1. Behavior can be *shaped* toward a specified goal by reinforcing successive, small steps toward the goal.

2. Shaping requires the therapist to break down the final goal into its discrete, constituent behaviors. In this process, reinforcement is given for accomplishing each step along the pathway to the final goal.

3. Reinforcing every correct response (continuous reinforcement) facilitates the acquisition of new behavior while reinforcing occasional correct responses (intermittent reinforcement) leads to behavior which is durable and resistant to extinction.

4. In shaping behavior, it is necessary to reinforce each step toward the goal enough times to ensure its stability. Reinforcing any one step too often, however, may result in behavior which becomes unchangeable, thus impeding the progress of the shaping procedure. Too frequent reinforcement may also result in satiation (*see* next Chapter).

5. Successful shaping requires careful attention and sensitivity to small changes in behavior. Shaping is an art as well as a science.

Chapter 5: EXTINCTION AND SATIATION

In the preceding chapters we have considered how desired behaviors can be increased or shaped by using response-contingent reinforcement. Many clinical problems involve an excess or surplus of undesired behavior; thus, we would like to have methods of eliminating already existing behavior. The next two chapters will focus on procedures which are effective in decreasing ongoing, maladaptive behavior.

The process of *extinction* occurs when a response is not reinforced and as a result decreases in frequency or intensity. After losing a few coins to a vending machine without obtaining the desired goody, we are less likely to "feed" the machine. If we have a friend who stops showing interest in our conversation or never accepts our invitation, we start looking for another friend. Many clinical applications have stemmed from the concept of extinction—a simple and basic experimental tactic. You will encounter some of the applications in Part II of this book, but let us examine one example now.

Miss Jones, a psychiatric patient hospitalized for seven years, had developed the habit of repeatedly coming to the nurses' station and complaining about her somatic symptoms, the condition of the ward, the treatment program, and about other patients she did not like. For a year or so, she consistently made ten to twenty visits to the nurses' station each day. She participated very little in the ongoing ward activities. The response of the nurses, whose work was being interrupted, was to irritably talk with Miss Jones, reassure her and finally order her to leave or even accompany her back to the day room. One nurse, in particular, spent more time pacifying Miss Jones and it was during this nurse's shift that most of the patient's visits to the office occurred.

While we might understand Miss Jones' frequent visits to the nurses' station being maintained by the attentive responses she obtained from the nurses (positive reinforcement), the important question is what to do to remedy the situation. Would you:

Instruct the nurses to completely ignore Miss Jones .... turn to page 89.

Instruct the nurses to ignore Miss Jones when she enters the nurses' station but show her interest and regard when she shows even the slightest involvement in ward activities .... turn to page 91.

Ignoring Miss Jones might eventually diminish her pestering, but it is likely that she would exhibit other disruptive behaviors in order to capture the attention she is accustomed to receiving from the staff.

Return to page 87 and choose the correct answer.

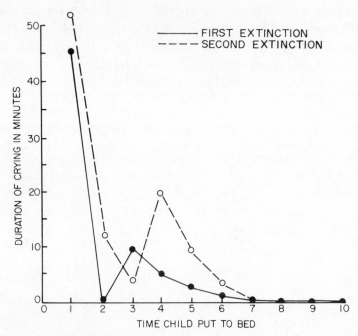

Fig 2. Length of crying in two extinction series as a function of successive occasions of being put to bed. (From Williams, C. D. The Elimination of Tantrum Behavior by Extinction procedures. *J. Abnorm. Soc. Psychol.*, 1959, **59**, 269. Reproduced by permission of the American Psychological Association.)

Ignoring maladaptive behavior, the process called extinction, can work by itself, particularly when it leaves the individual with alternate, adaptive behavior that can be easily reinforced. An example of this is a child's temper tantrums which occur at bedtime and necessitate long bed-side vigils by the parents. Figure 2 shows the extinction of bed-time tantrums in a 21-month-old child.

The first time the child was put to bed with the parents leaving the room and closing the door, the crying lasted 45 minutes. By the fifth time, the child was crying less than 5 minutes and by the tenth time he was smiling when the parents left. About a week later he screamed after his aunt put him to bed and she reinforced the tantrum by coming back and staying with him until he fell asleep. A second extinction was needed and is shown by the dotted line in the graph. With this extinction the crying terminated by the ninth occasion and no further tantrums were reported during the next two years (Williams, 1959).

Since sleep served as a reinforcer for the tired boy lying in bed quietly and because there was little opportunity for other activities, the extinction procedure alone could be used without side-effects.

In this case, two techniques are better than one. It might be possible to stop disruptive behavior by ignoring it but the patient, accustomed to a great deal of attention, may begin to exhibit other behaviors, very likely regressive ones, to re-capture the involvement of the staff. This does not inevitably occur (*see* page 90), but when it does happen we may find somebody like Miss Jones having temper tantrums, attacking staff members, destroying furniture, cutting her wrists, or becoming denudative. She is reverting to behaviors which perhaps had been reinforced at an earlier time in her life but which now seem grossly immature.

To prevent these undesirable side-effects, the staff should reinforce behavior that is adaptive *and* incompatible with the original disruptiveness. By paying particular attention to Miss Jones' efforts in ward meetings, occupational therapy, or hospital job these behaviors will increase and reduce the likelihood of regression.

A 20-year-old woman suffered from chronic neurodermatitis on the back of her neck. She scratched herself persistently despite the severe lesions and the extensive medical treatments she received. An analysis of the family situation revealed that the young woman with her skin complaints was able to garner most of her parents' attention from her younger brother, who had been in a preferred position in the family. In addition, she received a great deal of solicitous attention from her fiance who would frequently rub lotions and ointments on her neck.

A clinical hypothesis was formed to explain the scratching behavior on the basis of the large amounts of attention (social reinforcement) it was generating in significant others. The therapist got the cooperation of the family members and the fiance in discontinuing their concern and interest in the young woman's dermatitis. Soon thereafter the scratching decreased in frequency and within three months the dermatitis had completely cleared. A follow-up, four years later, found the woman without any recurrence of the dermatitis, happily married and productively employed (Walton, 1960).

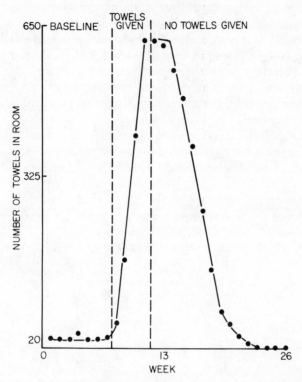

Fig. 3. Elimination of towel hoarding by a satiation procedure. (From Ayllon, T. Intensive Treatment of Psychotic Behaviour by Stimulus Satiation and Food Reinforcement. *Behaviour Research and Therapy*, 1963, **1**, 53–61.)

Another technique used to reduce the rate of maladaptive behavior is called *satiation*. Satiation occurs when a response decreases as a previously reinforcing stimulus is continued to be supplied. In the laboratory, an animal will cease working for food after a large amount of food has been eaten. The saying, "It's good to get away on a vacation, but it's always good to get home," refers to the satiation we experience when we have too much of a good thing on a holiday. The frequency of sexual behavior is also regulated by satiation—most couples reach some optimum rate of sexual intercourse after a decline from an initial burst of sex following marriage.

Satiation techniques have been applied to hoarding problems by Ayllon (1963). A patient who collected towels and kept 19–29 of them constantly in her room despite the efforts of nurses to retrieve them was given gradually increasing numbers of towels each day. By the third week of the procedure, she was receiving 60 towels a day and had accumulated 625 towels in her

room. At this point, the patient began removing the towels and the "rein-forcement" was stopped. Figure 3* illustrates the process and shows that the accumulated hoard disappeared over eleven weeks. During the next year only one to five towels were kept and a longer follow-up period revealed no return to hoarding nor appearance of any other problem behavior.

* Reprinted with permission of the author from T. Ayllon's Intensive Treatment of Psychotic Behavior by Stimulus Satiation and Food Reinforcement in the *Journal of Behaviour Research and Therapy*, Vol. 1, pp. 53–61, 1963. Copyright © 1963 by Pergamon Press. Additional information and related research are found in *The token economy: a motivational system for therapy and rehabilitation*, by T. Ayllon and N. H. Azrin, published by Appleton-Century-Crofts, New York, 1968.

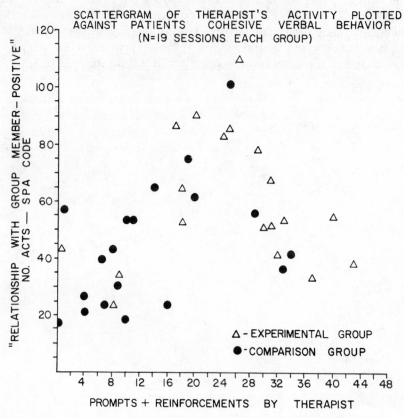

Fig. 4. Scattergram of therapist's activity plotted against patients' cohesive verbal behavior. (From Liberman, R. P. Unpublished data from a study on Behavioral Group Therapy.)

Another example of satiation which has direct relevance to the practice of psychotherapy is illustrated in Fig. 4. In this study of group psychotherapy, by the author, a satiation effect occurred in two separate groups when the therapists reinforced expressions of cohesiveness and solidarity among the group members. As the scattergram reflects, when either therapist provided more than 26 acknowledgements for this content category, the rate of cohesive expression declined.

The obvious implication for the conduct of psychotherapy is that overloading the patient(s) with acknowledgements, clarifications, or interpretations on any one issue may paradoxically lead to a reduction in the very behavior targeted for therapeutic strengthening.

SUMMARY OF CHAPTER 5

1. Extinction and satiation are useful methods for decreasing the rate or intensity of maladaptive behavior.

2. Extinction occurs when a learned response is no longer reinforced and consequently declines in frequency.

3. In clinical practice, it is advisable to couple extinction of maladaptive behavior with positive reinforcement of desired, adaptive behavior.

4. Satiation occurs when behavior decreases in frequency as a result of continued and super-abundant provision of a previously reinforcing stimulus.

Chapter 6: PUNISHMENT AND AVERSIVE CONDITIONING

The most common way of reducing the frequency of behavior is by punishment. While punishment has many culturally and ethically loaded connotations, we can define it as a behavioral procedure very simply. Punishment occurs when a behavior is weakened by an event which follows it in time. Spankings, then, are punishments only if they produce a reduction in the behavior on which they are contingent. You can see that this definition is a functional one that ties together the behavior and the aversive stimulus. However noxious it may seem from a cultural or even physical standpoint, a stimulus is not defined as a punisher by its intrinsic qualities, but rather in the effect the stimulus has on the preceding behavior. Only if a particular stimulus weakens or terminates behavior on which it is contingent is the process called punishment. As with reinforcement procedures punishment will be effective to the extent that the aversive stimulus follows the target behavior immediately in time.

Punishment is so often used as a practical mode of behavior control because it produces results fast. The undesirable behavior of a disobedient child is quickly suppressed by a whack on the backside. The person applying the punishment is negatively reinforced for using punishment because the bothersome disobedience ends. The teacher who sends the disrespectful and unruly student to the principal's office is reinforced because he can escape from the aversive qualities of the student's behavior. Because punishment procedures produce immediate suppression of unwanted and annoying behavior, they are used frequently and widely. They are the cornerstone of our legal system (imagine a policeman giving a reward to a motorist who stops at a red light) and pervade the educational, occupational and family systems.

However, unless exceedingly severe, punishment only temporarily suppresses unwanted behavior. In the absence of the punisher, undesirable behavior usually reappears; when there are no police cars, we are likely to exceed the speed limit. When the teacher steps out of the classroom, the noise level rises appreciably.

There are other disadvantages to the use of punishment procedures as the sole means of modifying behavior. These are undesirable side-effects of punishment such as emotional and aggressive behavior. Palpitations, sweating, contraction of muscles, and efforts to escape or strike back all can interfere with a program to shape behavior in more desirable directions.

A clinical example will help to clarify the distinction between punishment and negative reinforcement. Goldiamond (1965) has reported a remarkably effective method for the elimination of stuttering. After obtaining baseline rates of stuttering, the therapist introduces delayed auditory feedback through headphones to the client. The feedback is an aversive stimulus as anyone will attest who has tried to carry on a conversation while simultaneously hearing the speech he uttered 250 milliseconds previously. The delayed auditory feedback is presented contingent upon the occurrence of stuttering responses. The client is given the responsibility to define his own stuttering and to administer the noxious feedback to himself under the therapist's supervision. In order to avoid the delayed feedback, the stutterer must slow down his speech. As this happens, the disfluencies disappear. The client's fluent but abnormally slowed speech is then gradually increased in speed by mechanically pacing the reading material. At the same time, the delayed auditory feedback is faded out. Goldiamond has reported 100 per cent success in each of 45 clients and describes procedures which assist the client to generalize their laboratory-based fluency to natural settings.

The presentation of delayed auditory feedback is a *punishment* procedure because it results in the *decrease* and eventual elimination of stuttering responses. At the same time, fluent speech is *negatively reinforced*; that is, by speaking fluently, the client can *avoid* the aversive feedback. Stuttering is punished (decreased) and fluency is negatively reinforced (increased).

Punishment should be distinguished from negative reinforcement. The initiate to behavior principles can be easily confused by these very different principles. In punishment, the targeted behavior *decreases* as a result of the contingent application of an aversive stimulus. On the other hand, negative reinforcement *increases* the targeted behavior because the behavior enables the individual to escape or avoid an aversive stimulus or event. You can see that punishment procedures would be used to eliminate unwanted behavior while negative reinforcement procedures would be useful for facilitating desired behavior. Frequently, both principles are operating in the same treatment approach.

Aversive stimuli have been used to control the disabling problem called "writer's cramp." The cramp is a combination of tremors and spasms of hand muscles which prevent legible writing in those whose work requires a great deal of writing. In one study (Sylvester & Liversedge, 1960), 39 cases of writer's cramp were treated with a procedure that aimed at decreasing the tremors and spasms by response-contingent shock. A number of the clients had undergone psychotherapy with little or no improvement of their symptoms and they did not appear to share common personality traits.

Tremors were punished by having the clients insert a stylus into a series of progressively smaller holes—whenever the stylus hit the side of the hole, a painful but harmless shock was delivered. Spasms were dealt with in a similar fashion. An electrified pen yielded shock if excessive pressure was applied by the patient's hand. In addition, the clients were required to write designated line patterns on a metal plate. If they strayed from the pattern, which was similar to normal writing pattern, they received a shock.

After 3 to 6 weeks of treatment, 24 of the 39 clients showed satisfactory writing and were able to resume their work. When these people were interviewed four and a half years later, they were found to have maintained their improvement. Five clients improved with the training but later relapsed.

One of the oldest forms of behavior therapy, aversion therapy, is based on the effectiveness of punishment. Alcoholics, drug addicts, and sexual deviates have been the clinical groups primarily exposed to this type of treatment.

Mr. Diamond was a 26-year-old narcotic addict who volunteered for aversion therapy while hospitalized. The procedure used to weaken Mr. Diamond's use of narcotics:

A. Consisted of a painful electric shock delivered to his arm just prior to his injecting himself with an opiate .... turn to page 107.

B. Consisted of the onset of apomorphine-induced nausea and retching immediately following his injecting himself with an opiate.... turn to page 105.

Two boys who had a masturbatory fetish involving ladies' underwear were given aversion therapy. They frequently stole panties, bras, and slips from clotheslines and had been apprehended by the police. An assortment of 20 different women's underclothes was assembled and combined with 20 items of clothing that were non-fetishistic. The boys were presented the various items in random order and were given brief electric shocks intermittently when they held the fetishistic items.

After several sessions, the boys indicated that they were no longer attracted by female underwear. They stopped their raids on clotheslines and gave up their fetish (Bond & Evans, 1967).

An aversive stimulus, such as apomorphine-induced nausea and retching, appiied immediately after a problem behavior can be defined as a punishment procedure if a decrease in the problem behavior is produced. Two pilot studies (Liberman, 1968; Raymond, 1964) suggest that such a decrease does occur.

But because of the drawbacks of punishment procedures used alone, behavior therapists have tended to couple aversion therapy with reinforcement of alternate, more adaptive responses. Thus, in the case of a drug addict, during certain experimental trials the patient could avoid receiving apomorphine if he chose a bottle of soda, some candy and cigarettes instead of the opiate-loaded syringe. In addition to the avoidance of the nausea and the enjoyment of the food and smoking, the patient was able to amiably converse with his therapist.

In a later section on the behavior therapy of autistic children, we will hear about other applications of punishment paired with reinforcement of more adaptive behavior. It is clear that punishment used to suppress unwanted behavior when combined with reinforcement of more appropriate behavior is a most powerful therapeutic approach.

Perhaps we should repeat that the definition of a punishment procedure entails the application of an aversive stimulus immediately *following* the unwanted behavior. Backward conditioning, illustrated by Mr. Diamond receiving an electric shock *prior* to the unwanted behavior, is not effective in suppressing the problem behavior.

Go back to page 103 and choose the correct answer.

A fundamental principle of learning is that an individual's behavior is governed and motivated by the consequences it produces in his environment. Consequences which increase the behavior they are contingent upon are called *positive reinforcers* (rewards). When behavior is increased because it enables an individual to avoid or escape certain consequences, such consequences are termed *negative reinforcers* (aversive stimuli). *Punishment* occurs when a negative reinforcer suppresses or weakens behavior on which it is contingent. When behavior decreases in frequency or intensity because it does not meet with reinforcement, the process is called *extinction*.

From the point of view of a clinician interested in methods to increase adaptive behavior and decrease maladaptive behavior, positive and negative reinforcement increase the likelihood of behavior occurring while punishment and extinction decrease the likelihood of its occurrence. The following table organizes the functional relationships between an individual's behavior and the consequences it generates in his environment.

		Behavior Increases	Behavior Decreases
Consequences	Behavior Produces Stimulus	Positive Reinforcement (rewarding stimulus)	Punishment (aversive stimulus)
	Behavior Avoids Stimulus	Negative Reinforcement (aversive stimulus)	Extinction (no stimulus)

SUMMARY OF CHAPTER 6

1. Technically, only if a particular stimulus or event *weakens or stops* the behavior on which it focuses is the process called *punishment*.

2. The same aversive or noxious stimulus or event which can be used to suppress undesirable behavior through punishment, can also be used to *negatively reinforce* (increase) behavior which succeeds in escaping or avoiding it.

3. Punishment produces reduction in unwanted behavior quickly and reliably, but the results are frequently temporary and accompanied by emotional side-effects.

4. It is most efficacious to combine punishment of maladaptive behavior with reinforcement of desired behavior. While the pathological behavior is suppressed by punishment, alternate responses can be established and made durable by reinforcement.

Chapter 7: GENERALIZATION AND DISCRIMINATION

Generalization of learning occurs when a behavior we have learned in one setting appears in another setting. If humans (or animals) did not possess the capacity to generalize their learning to new stimulus situations, our behavioral repertoires would be exceedingly constricted and we would have to go through the tedious process of acquiring new responses in each new situation we found ourselves. Generalization occurs according to a number of laws which have been worked out with animals under laboratory conditions. One of these laws deals with the similarity of a novel setting to the setting in which a response was originally learned. The greater the similarity between the stimulus characteristics of the two settings, the greater the likelihood that generalization will occur.

We can observe the process of generalization when a child is learning to use language. At first the child will speak only at home in response to certain prompts from particular people, usually his parents. As time goes on, the child will talk in response to other people and in places other than his home. The same child might say, "Daddy," in response to seeing many different men or "Bow-wow" in response to seeing a cat.

When stimuli share attributes in common, generalization of a response may occur. A person who learns how to drive one kind of car can generalize his "driving behavior" to other types of cars. The more similar the cars, the quicker the generalization. It may take some extra lessons to change from a car with an automatic transmission to one with a clutch and stick shift.

In clinical situations, the process of generalization becomes a crucial determinant of therapeutic outcome. Transfer or generalization of learning from the therapy situation to the real-life situation must occur for treatment to succeed.

An important step in any behavior therapy procedure is the final one of carrying over treatment effects to the natural environment. The beneficial changes in a pupil's behavior in a special classroom where he has the extra attention of a teacher and a programmed curriculum with clear, consistent and immediate contingencies of reinforcement must eventually transfer to the regular classroom. Generalization of treatment effects must also occur from psychiatric settings to the real world outside. At the Clinical Research Unit at Camarillo State Hospital, we have developed a gradual fading procedure which maximizes the probability of transfer of effects.

Patients are admitted to the Unit from other wards around the hospital or from community mental health centers for individualized, intensive behavior modification programs. They have failed to respond to previous, conventional treatment efforts. After a therapy approach is found to be effective, generalization is promoted back to their "home ward" or community setting by:

1. Gradually fading the Clinical Research Unit and its personnel out of the picture by having the patient spend more and more time in his other setting.
2. Having the Research Unit personnel accompany the patient for visits back to his previous setting.
3. Bringing the therapists from the patient's previous setting into the Clinical Research Unit and giving them training in continuing the treatment methods after transfer has occurred.

The psychoanalytic concept of transference can be described as an example of stimulus generalization. The patient responds to the analyst as though he were a parent. The analyst shares some of the same stimulus characteristics as does the patient's parent—he is an authority figure, respected, knowledgeable, concerned and interested in the patient, and sympathetic. The less the patient learns about the actual characteristics of the analyst, the greater the chance for generalization or transference. Hence transference will more likely occur in analysis than in therapy. Much of the process of psychoanalysis focuses on the working through the transference which entails teaching the patient how he is confusing early life figures with the analyst. Thus, as analysis proceeds, generalization first increases and then decreases. Part of the notion of "transference cure" derives from the supportive and healing properties of the patient responding to a therapist who resembles an earlier nurturant figure.

The closer the treatment situation resembles the client's natural environment, the greater is the chance for the treatment effects to "take." In the treatment of depression, some behavior therapists (Lewinsohn *et al.*, 1969) have gone directly into the patient's home to make a behavioral analysis of the problem and then to modify the maladaptive patterns of interaction which maintain the depressive behavior.

> On the basis of the home observations, the therapist identifies those interpersonal behavior patterns which he assumes to be causally related to the depression. These findings are presented to the client and his spouse over several interviews . . . behavioral goals are agreed upon . . . the home visits immediately focus the therapist–client interaction on behavioral and interpersonal problems and they constitute an easy way of involving a significant part of the client's environment in the treatment process.*

Treatment is carried out by changing the contingencies of interpersonal response within the family, with all members of the family collaborating in the effort, including the person designated as the patient. Figure 5 shows the results of one case with the change in symptoms reflected by the Depression Adjective Checklist.

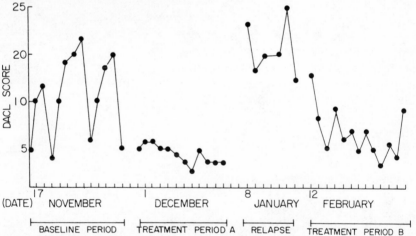

Fig. 5. Behavioral modification of depressive behavior with home treatment. (From Lewinsohn, Peter M., Weinstein, Malcolm S., & Shaw, David A. Depression: A Clinical-Research Approach. In R. Rubin (Ed.), *Advances in behavior therapy*, Vol. 1. Copyright Academic Press, New York, 1969.)

---

* Reprinted with permission of the authors and Academic Press, New York, from P. M. Lewinsohn, M. Weinstein, and D. Shaw's Depression: A clinical-research approach, in R. Rubin and C. M. Franks (Eds.) *Advances in behavior modification*, Vol. I, 1969. Copyright © 1969 by Academic Press.

114

The behavior therapist consciously and systematically constructs the treatment setting to be as similar as possible to the natural environment in which the patient's problem occurs. If, for example, a patient is having difficulty asserting himself in a work situation, the therapist might choose to engage in role-playing various encounters at work. Giving the patient actual opportunity to try out and rehearse the new behavior in a *situation which closely resembles the real-life situation* will facilitate the transfer of learning.

In aversion therapy of narcotic addicts, the author (Liberman, 1968) arranged for the patients to use their usual injection implements (their "works") in the treatment situation. The aversive stimulus (nausea from apomorphine) was thereby paired with the very objects (e.g., necktie tourniquet) which would be used outside the hospital by the addict. This would increase the likelihood of generalization of the aversive experience from treatment to home neighborhood.

Family therapy capitalizes on stimulus generalization by bringing the day-to-day important relationships directly into the treatment setting. While family members will behave somewhat differently in the presence of the therapist and in the clinic office than they do at home, the jump in transferring learning is less demanding here than in individual therapy. For this reason alone, family therapy is potentially more effective than individual therapy—particularly when the problems are imbedded in the family interaction. After a while in therapy, the therapist becomes more familiar, less alien, and the family members usually interact more spontaneously and naturally. Some family therapists have even described their being incorporated into the family in some fashion. Other workers with families go directly into the home to make their observations and perform the therapy.

Another example of the exploitation of the principle of generalization is a treatment program for alcoholics at Patton State Hospital in California (Schaefer, 1969). The method used is aversive therapy with the alcoholics receiving painful but harmless electric shocks to their fingers when they take a sip of liquor. The shock is turned off when the patient spits out the liquor. The chances that the treatment will generalize to the community are enhanced by constructing the therapeutic milieu as a typical tavern, complete with bar, stools, jukebox, and bartender (a nurse in disguise).

The process complementary to generalization is called discrimination. When we emit a response in one situation, but not in a different situation, we are exhibiting discrimination. This comes about by our being reinforced for showing behavior in one setting, but not being reinforced in another setting. This process of differential reinforcement enables us to learn to act in ways appropriate to the situation. We can uninterruptedly enjoy eating our picnic lunch with our fingers, but we will draw stares and possibly censure if we use our fingers to eat in a posh restaurant. You may win applause and trophies if you bear down hard in a tennis competition, but similarly intense play with your spouse would earn only anger or hurt feelings. We can drive at 60 mph on the highway but will slow down to 20 mph in the city. We raise our voices at a baseball game but whisper in a library. We use formal language while giving a lecture but unless we change our speaking style with friends we may be viewed as pompous. We dress casually on the beach but more formally when we go for a job interview. When different consequences follow our behavior in different settings, we learn to discriminate. Since our becoming social beings depends upon our making differential responses appropriate to various interpersonal settings, discrimination learning is a pervasive and central process in our lives.

Some people can make finer discriminations than others because of their history of differential reinforcement. Dog fanciers can distinguish many different breeds of canines. Asians can discriminate among many more types of rice than Europeans. Expert wine tasters are paid to make distinctions among vintages. Professional musicians can distinguish musical tones better than a layman. We can multiply these examples a thousandfold since we are constantly making discriminations in daily life.

Much of our behavior is under the control of situational stimuli or cues called *discriminative stimuli*. We press the accelerator when the light turns green, but press the brake when the light turns red. We are likely to shake hands with a friend we meet on the street but not with a stranger. We smile in response to another person's smile but not to his smirk. Rules of etiquette and diplomatic protocol are based on the principle of stimulus discrimination. When we behave differently toward individuals possessing different religious or racial characteristics we are literally "discriminating." Laws which are passed to ensure civil liberties and equality of opportunity attempt to eliminate discrimination by attaching certain negative consequences to this behavior.

We must take the process of discrimination into account in our work with patients. Teaching a patient to vary his behavior according to the situation is a cornerstone of any therapy. The schizophrenic is diagnosed as such in part because his affective and social behavior is inappropriate to the situation. During the course of hospitalization, the ward staff gives differential feedback (reinforcement) to the psychotic patient to help him bring his behavior under

The control that stimuli have over behavior can produce interesting and important clinical problems. This is particularly so when the stimulus control emanates from a significant person in the patient's life space. The following case vignette (Moser, 1965) illustrates how a young autistic boy responded to human discriminative stimuli in a striking fashion:

> Whenever her husband was home, Billy was a model youngster. He knew that his father would punish him quickly and dispassionately for misbehaving. But when his father left the house, Billy would go to the window and watch until the car pulled out. As soon as it did, he was suddenly transformed. . . . "He'd go into my closet and tear up my evening dresses and urinate on my clothes. He'd smash furniture and run around biting the walls until the house was destruction from one end to the other." [p. 96]

Billy's father served as a discriminative stimulus for certain punitive consequences to destructive behavior. His mother in the home alone was a discriminative stimulus which signified no punishment for this sort of rampant behavior. In fact, Billy received concern and intense attention from his mother when he acted up in this manner. When behavior is met with different consequences in the presence of different people, a child can learn to discriminate the signalling meanings of each person's presence.

How would you go about improving the situation at Billy's house?

the appropriate stimulus controls. If he is denudative or combative, he will be placed in the quiet room. If he talks rationally with the staff, he will receive their interest and attention. The process of group therapy consists of a great deal of discriminative learning of social behavior. A group member's actions during therapy is met with differential responses by the other members and the therapist and is gradually shaped toward more prosocial form. When we attach different consequences, positive and negative, to the overt or reported behavior of our patients we are involved in the process of discrimination training.

SUMMARY OF CHAPTER 7

1. To exploit the process of *generalization*, the behavior therapist systematically constructs the treatment setting to be as similar as possible to the natural environment in which the patient's problem occurs.

2. When different consequences follow our behavior in different settings, we learn to *discriminate* by changing our behavior accordingly. Stimuli or settings which signal the contingencies of reinforcement that are operating give us cues that enable us to modify or modulate our behavior and make it appropriate to the situation. These cues are called *discriminative stimuli*.

3. Because we are social beings, the most important discriminative stimuli for human behavior derive from people. Laughs, smiles, handshakes, frowns, and fists are examples of discriminative stimuli.

Chapter 8: IMITATIVE LEARNING

A large portion of our behavioral repertoires comes into being, not by the shaping of *spontaneous* responses into elaborate sequences or chains of behavior, but by the reinforcement of imitated responses. If many of our complex patterns of behavior had to be built up by tedious trial and error, parents and children, teachers and students would be exhausted before much progress occurred. We have the capacity, however, of incorporating long chains of responses wholesale into our accumulated experience simply by observing someone else making these responses. Imitative or observational learning plays a part in the acquisition of such behaviors as swinging a golf club or tennis racquet, running an electric saw, and peeling a potato. Adding words to our vocabulary, changing a hairdo or a style of dress, and voting for the same political party as our parents are all examples of imitative or observational learning. As we shall see, this type of learning, a process which has long been termed identification, plays an important part in psychotherapy.

A number of factors combine to influence the probability that behavior shown by a model will be reproduced by the observer. One of the most important factors is whether or not the observer sees the model get reinforcement for the modeled response. A child is much less likely to imitate a bully's aggressive behavior if the bully is punished than if he gets away with it. Another factor is how powerful or prestigious the model is viewed by the observer. High status people tend to be imitated much more often than low status people. The advertising industry has exploited this principle of social learning by hiring celebrities to act in commercials. Individuals who are seen as having access to a wide variety of rewards, thus, are much more effective models.

Two factors which have been experimentally found to favorably influence the rate and degree of imitation are the (1) similarity between model and observer and (2) the possession by the observer of components of the response to be emulated. Behavior is more readily imitated when an individual has already established in his repertoire behavioral elements or rudiments that can be tied together to form the more complex act that is being modeled. These two factors may help to account for the ineffectiveness of middle-class therapists in their work with clients who come from a lower social class or different racial group.

Perhaps the most important factor which determines the sustaining of modeled behavior is the presence of reinforcement, incentives or social sanctions for the imitator. In an interesting experiment, Bandura (1969) showed that children who viewed adult models being rewarded for physical and verbal aggression were much more likely to imitate aggression than other children who viewed the same adults being punished for exhibiting the same behavior. However, when incentives were provided to the children for expressing aggression, both groups of children showed much higher and equivalent levels of aggression.

The above principles have been applied to clinical problems with success. In a classic experiment, Jones (1924) demonstrated that children who were fearful of a rabbit could be "cured" of their phobia by having them observe other children fearlessly approach and handle the rabbit. Forty years later, this work was replicated by Bandura and his colleagues (Bandura, 1969). He taught children who were afraid of dogs to become unafraid by watching a non-anxious child go through steps of gradually increasing degrees of contact with the dog, becoming gradually bolder in contact with the dog.

Observational or imitative learning plays an important part in many settings of clinical teaching and practice in psychiatry.

In each of the following settings, indicate how modeling or imitation takes place.

1. A therapeutic milieu where recently admitted patients are mixed together with those ready for discharge.
2. Teaching interviewing technique through a one-way mirror.
3. Group psychotherapy.
4. Recruitment of psychiatric residents for psychoanalytic training.

Rehearse your answer by yourself before turning to page 129 for a discussion of the above items.

Sonny was a 6½-year-old boy who had been hospitalized for three years with the diagnosis of autism. Psychotherapy had failed to alter his bizarre habits of playing with his fingers, spitting, and ritualistically manipulating toys. He was completely mute and made no sounds whatsoever.

For 21 days Sonny was intensively treated by means of a combined imitative and reinforcement approach. During six hours of daily training, food, water and relief from physical restraint (all paired with verbal approval) were used to reinforce Sonny's efforts at imitating the therapist's appropriate use of his body, objects, and vocalizations.

After the training period, Sonny was able to imitate over 200 responses including making facial expressions, jumping, picking up a scissors and using it correctly, drawing, throwing and catching a ball, brushing his teeth, appropriately using toys, and pounding nails with a hammer. He consistently imitated 18 sounds and 18 words. Expansion and generalization of the therapeutic effects were effected by teaching the ward staff and his parents in using imitation and reinforcement techniques. Five months after the start of therapy, Sonny had increased his performance beyond mere imitation. He was able to print the alphabet, throw a basketball through a hoop, and name over 200 objects and pictures. He could say simple sentences and answer questions (Hingtgen *et al.*, 1967).

Therapeutic communities in which patients at various stages of functioning or recovery live together contain rich and varied opportunities for imitative learning. The more regressed patients can observe the better put-together patients in their round of activities and see how the latter's progress is met with approval and the granting of privileges by the staff. The extent to which patients possess elements of improved functioning in their premorbid repertoires, are from similar backgrounds and age groupings, and receive incentives or reinforcements for their attempts to imitate, all govern the rapidity of the vicarious learning process. Of course the learning can proceed in the opposite direction such as when well-functioning patients emulate (act out) their more regressed counterparts who may be receiving a great deal of attention and interest from the staff.

Learning how to do psychotherapy or interviewing by watching models behind a one-way screen or on videotape has become a popular didactic method. The principles involved are largely based on the potentialities for vicarious or imitative learning. These methods might be improved by using models who have had similar experiences as the observer (e.g., residents watching residents), providing differential reinforcement for the models as they approximate better technique, or having high status figures serve as models. It is of interest to note that a group of black psychiatrists have recently protested the prevalence of white, middle-class psychiatrists teaching black residents and the inappropriateness of these instructors as models or ego-ideals.

Group psychotherapy provides frequent opportunities for "silent" members to learn from more active and verbal members, ways of coping with and adapting to interpersonal problems. If learning occurred only when patients in a group were talking or being focused on by the therapist, the effectiveness of the technique would be diminished greatly. Group therapists have often experienced a heretofore quiet and withdrawn member suddenly exhibit behavior which had been modeled by others in the group.

It is clear that young psychiatrists who are trained in centers where the most prestigious and admired supervisors and senior staff are analysts much more often decide upon psychoanalytic training than their peers in residency programs where psychoanalysts are not accorded high status.

This discussion does not exhaust the modeling mechanism operating in each of the above four situations. What other clinical settings contain elements of imitative learning?

A combination of imitation and guided participation or practice was used to treat acrophobics. The therapist demonstrated the climbing of increasing heights to the patients. The patients were then physically assisted by the therapist (by accompanying them) to carry out the same climbing responses. This occurred during a single 35-minute session. After the session, the patients were given a behavioral test requiring them to climb to a series of heights on top of a seven-story building. Modeling combined with guided practice produced greater changes than modeling alone or modeling combined with the therapist verbally guiding the patients in their practice. Similar results have been obtained in patients afraid of snakes. Research has demonstrated that 60 percent of the overall beneficial effects of such combined procedures stems from the modeling part and the remainder from guided participation (Bandura, 1969, pp. 189–191).

SUMMARY OF CHAPTER 8

1. Imitation or modeling occurs when an individual acquires new behavior by observing other people's behavior and its consequences.

2. Imitation proceeds best when:

   a. The model has status (i.e., has access to rewards).

   b. The model has power (i.e., can give rewards).

   c. The model is reinforced for the exemplified behavior.

   d. The model is similar to the observer.

   e. The observer has the components of the modeled behavior already in his repertoire.

   f. The observer has a chance to practice the behavior soon after watching the model.

   g. The observer is reinforced himself for performing the modeled behavior.

3. Vicarious extinction of emotional behavior can occur with therapeutic outcome by exposing an observer to a model who approaches object or situation feared by the observer with calmness and positive expression.

4. An individual can achieve lasting and generalized reductions in avoidance behavior based on fear through observing a model. The beneficial effects also can spread to other feared situations not specifically included in the treatment program.

Part II

Behavior Therapy at Work

This section will describe the methods currently being used by behavior therapists to successfully treat a number of psychiatric problems. The earlier sections have provided you with the orientation and concepts necessary to understand these methods. Although the techniques in use vary greatly in their specifics, they all have the following in common:

a. Derivation from the principles of experimental psychology, learning theory, and conditioning.
b. Focus on observable behavior.
c. Achievement of empirical results.

Because behavior therapists focus on successful outcome rather than success in applying the process of treatment, they strive for flexibility and are open to the invention of new techniques. As a result, the field of behavior therapy is subject to continuous experimental modification. To keep abreast of innovations, you can consult the pages of the four behavior therapy journals— *Behavior Research and Therapy, Journal of Applied Behavioral Analysis, Behavior Therapy*, and the *Journal of Behavior Therapy and Experimental Psychiatry*. An annotated bibliography of source books and articles in behavior therapy is presented for your convenience at the end of the book.

Indicative of the healthy infancy of behavior therapies is the fact that from the start they have diverged in their methods and taken their theoretical underpinnings from several different models of learning and conditioning. These theories serve to stimulate therapeutic practice with new strategies, not to constrict practice in ideological straightjackets. In this part of the book we will focus directly upon some of the practical methods being used to modify clinically relevant behavior.

Clinical efforts are bolstered by a condition that is common to all therapies that work—a trusting therapist–patient relationship. The extent to which the therapist–patient relationship plays a role in the treatment process varies according to the specific technique being applied. However, we can say with assurance that a positive relationship—one suffused with mutual respect, warm regard, and collaboration—always beneficially affects the particular method being used. This benefit comes from the social reinforcement value for the patient of whatever the therapist says and does. The notion of the therapist's social reinforcement value has been recognized by non-behavior therapists and has been variously called the "therapeutic alliance," the "placebo effect," or "positive transference." As we shall see, the behavior therapist is not only aware of this condition but makes explicit use of it to facilitate therapeutic results.

Chapter 9: BEHAVIOR THERAPY WITH NEUROTICS: SYSTEMATIC DESENSITIZATION

Phobias and other avoidance problems based on anxiety have been successfully dealt with by a technique called "systematic desensitization." Desensitization was developed by a psychiatrist, Joseph Wolpe (1958, 1966, 1969), who is one of the pioneers of behavior therapy. The method proceeds by eliminating anxiety attached to feared situations through learning a response—deep muscle relaxation—which is incompatible with anxiety. Various therapists have reported marked to complete recovery in 72–90 percent of cases treated with desensitization in both controlled and uncontrolled studies.

After several initial interviews during which a history is taken and the problem is specified, the patient is taught how to deeply relax his voluntary muscles. Detailed instructions on how this is done can be found elsewhere (Wolpe & Lazarus, 1966). For now it will suffice to say that the therapist instructs the patient to alternately tighten (flex) and relax each muscle group in the body until the patient can discriminate the difference in feelings between contracted and relaxed muscles. Relaxation can be also accomplished using hypnosis or a short-acting barbiturate like methohexital (Brevital). After 2–4 sessions of training, when the patient has mastered deep muscle relaxation, the therapist delivers the anxiety-provoking stimuli, in a graded way, through verbal imagery. The patient is asked to imagine the physical and interpersonal dimensions of scenes while deeply relaxed.

A hierarchy of such scenes is constructed collaboratively by the therapist and patient with an emphasis on a stepwise progression from least to most anxiety-provoking. The hierarchy must be individualized for each patient. The patient is instructed to signal if he becomes anxious or tense during the presentation of any one item on the hierarchy. The therapist will then stop immediately, and go back to an earlier step in the hierarchy until relaxation is regained. At this point, progression through the hierarchy resumes.

Each scene is presented for two seconds or longer depending upon the stage of progression and the ability of the patient to respond to the therapist's verbal prompt with imagery. In general, each scene is presented 3 or 4 times and the duration of presentation should be briefer with the first one or two presentations. In the 10 to 50 seconds between presenting scenes, it is helpful to remind the patient to relax, especially the particular muscles which tend to be tense for him.

The scenes are described as graphically and true to life as possible to maximize the imagery and the generalization of the effects outside the office. The patient is instructed to pace himself in real life according to his progress through the hierarchy in the office. In some situations this may be practically impossible and it can be expected that progress will be slower. By the time all of the anxiety-evoking scenes in the hierarchy have been imagined with the patient maintaining deep relaxation, the patient should be free of significant anxiety in the real-life situations. The success of this procedure depends upon the occurrence of stimulus generalization. The more graphically similar the imagined scenes are to the real-life situations, and the better the patient is able to picture the scenes, the more therapeutic change will occur.

In addition, as the patient progresses stepwise through the hierarchy and completes a scene without tension, the therapist can *positively reinforce* successful relaxation by saying something like, "Good," . . . or "Fine, you're doing nicely." Social reinforcement from the therapist, in this way, helps to cement the progress being made by the patient as he substitutes relaxation for anxiety in the conditioning process.

Extinction also occurs since the scenes which previously elicited anxiety no longer do so. In other words, the patient is given an opportunity to reality test his irrational fear. By the use of imagery, the therapist engineers a situation which previously produced an avoidance response in the patient. Because of relaxation, however, the avoidance does not occur and the patient can directly experience that nothing aversive or calamitous ensues. Being exposed to a situation where the expected aversive stimulus does not occur, the patient's anxiety and avoidance behavior is weakened.

Besides the extinction going on at a "reflex" level, the patient is undergoing extinction on a verbal level since each time a scene is completed without experiencing anxiety, the patient places the label, "no anxiety" or "feel comfortable," on his imagined presence in that scene.

Desensitization, because of its systematic and carefully defined steps, has been automated to provide a self-administered experience. A number of research studies have shown that self-desensitization is as effective as treatment given by a "live" therapist. In automated desensitization, the individual is guided by a tape or phonograph recording through relaxation training, hierarchy construction, and the pairing of the relaxation with the previously anxiety-evoking scenes. A commercially available, self-desensitization program for anxiety taking tests can be obtained from the author.

In summary, the steps for carrying out systematic desensitization are as follows:

1. Gathering information about the problem through a detailed psychiatric history, with emphasis on the specific what, how much, where, with whom, and when of the problem.
2. Training the patient in deep muscle relaxation.
3. Constructing a detailed, step-by-step hierarchy or list of anxiety-evoking scenes in collaboration with the patient.
4. Counterposing relaxation against the anxiety-evoking scenes in a graded progression through the hierarchy.

Desensitization of anxiety occurs when the patient's deep muscular relaxation overrides the anxiety previously associated with certain situations. It is "systematic" because the patient moves step-by-step through a graded series of anxiety-evoking scenes until the anxiety has been counter-conditioned.

Below you will find two stimulus hierarchies which are out of proper order. In the spaces provided, re-arrange the items so they sequentially proceed from least to most anxiety-evoking (top to bottom).

Hierarchy for Frigidity		Hierarchy for Test Anxiety	
Embracing with husband	————	A month before exam	————
Breasts fondled through dress	————	Two days before exam	————
Seeing husband's penis	————	Cramming night before exam	————
Undressing with husband	————	Exam being distributed	————
Feeling penis on thigh	————	A week before exam	————
Lying together clothed	————	Walking to exam	————
Going into bedroom	————	Studying 4 days before exam	————
Penis fully inserted	————	Morning of exam	————
Lying together nude	————	Reading 1st question on exam	————
Penis touching vagina	————	Entering exam room	————
Petting each other nude	————	Answering questions on exam	————
Full sexual intercourse	————		
Holding hands on couch	————		

Turn to page 145 to check your answers with properly arranged hierarchies.

A behavioral technique related to desensitization called *implosion therapy* (Stampfl & Levis, 1968) is designed to bring the phobic patient into contact with the feared stimuli. The principle of this method is that if a patient can experience the anxiety and then experience its dissipation through reality-testing, the phobia will lose its motivational support (extinction). Sometimes contact with the stimuli is made directly and sometimes indirectly using imagery induced by suggestions. The goal is to elicit as much anxiety as possible and to continue presenting cues until a marked decrease in anxiety evocation occurs. For instance, a spider phobic would be asked to imagine that he was alone in a room in which there were numerous black hairy spiders which crawled up his legs and bit him and entered his nose while he screamed helplessly. The therapist maintains a running commentary on the scenes while the patient imagines for the full session, which usually lasts 30–60 minutes. The therapist follows a hypothesis by choosing cues which are part of the total conditioned stimulus complex. Theoretically, the closer the cues match the real-life aversive stimuli the greater will be the induced anxiety and the potential for extinction will increase. Many of the cues found to be effective in implosive therapy have been of psychodynamic interest—such as guilt, sexual conflicts, fears of bodily injury or rejection, and expression of aggression.

The rationale behind the method is much the same as for systematic desensitization: The patient persists in maladaptive patterns of avoidance or defenses because their continued performance prevents much of the motivating source of anxiety from being exposed and tested against reality. Without coming into contact with the feared stimuli, there is no chance for extinction to occur. The difference between desensitization and implosion is in the manner in which the feared stimuli are presented; gradually and with concurrent relaxation to counteract anxiety in the former but with full blast and repeatedly trying to induce anxiety in the latter. A report comparing the relative efficacy of these two approaches suggests that implosion may be more effective for agoraphobics (Marks *et al.*, 1970).

Hierarchy for Frigidity	*Hierarchy for Test Anxiety*
Holding hands on couch.	A month before exam.
Embracing with husband.	A week before exam.
Breasts fondled through dress.	Studying 4 days before exam.
Going into bedroom.	Two days before exam.
Lying together clothed.	Cramming night before exam.
Undressing with husband.	Morning of exam.
Seeing husband's penis.	Walking to exam.
Lying together nude.	Entering exam room.
Petting each other nude.	Exam being distributed.
Feeling penis on thigh.	Reading 1st question on exam.
Penis touching vagina.	Answering questions on exam.
Penis fully inserted.	
Full sexual intercourse.	

There are no "standard" hierarchies. Each patient requires a custom-made list of items which graphically portray his own anxiety-evoking problems. Particularly with the sexual sphere, individual idiosyncrasies with the various situations make impossible any absolute or constant hierarchy. The arrangement of adjacent steps will vary from person to person. Some patients can proceed through a brief hierarchy quickly while others require lengthy and detailed lists which they move through with deliberation and in tiny steps. If a therapist reaches an impasse with desensitization, one way to resolve the block is to break down the steps into sub-steps and thereby reduce the anxiety increment. In the frigidity example above, instead of an item "petting each other nude" several items could be substituted such as, "having face and neck kissed," "kissing each other's ears," "touching each other's thighs," "breasts fondled," "breasts kissed," and "vagina caressed."

Desensitization should not be used in cook-book fashion for every problem containing anxiety or avoidance components. Before commencing a course of desensitization, the clinician must work out a behavioral analysis of the problem and together with the patient decide upon rational goals for the therapy. In some cases, anxiety stems from symbolic rather than manifest situations. For instance, a patient with a fear of falling asleep may require a hierarchy around the issue of death and dying. Someone fearful of being in crowds and social occasions may actually be afraid of scrutiny, criticism or rejection by others. We must remember that man is a symbol-manipulating species. Higher cognitive processes play a phylogenetically important role in human behavior and will be involved in any behavior therapy to a greater or lesser degree. The future task is to identify these cognitive and symbolic processes and to evaluate how they interact with environmental events to influence behavior. In desensitization the hierarchy must involve the actual source of anxiety, hence the "meaning" of the feared stimuli to the patient must be considered.

In other cases, anxiety should not be tempered with relaxation but rather overcome with a more socially appropriate response such as assertiveness. An example of this would be a man who feels anxious at work when his co-workers intimidate him. Assertive training (*see* Chapter 10), not desensitization, is the treatment of choice. At times both desensitization and assertive training can be combined for maximal effectiveness such as in the case of a person who is afraid to speak out in social situations. Even if a person has "true" anxiety in social situations, if he does not have the relevant verbal and social responses in his repertoire (perhaps never having learned them) all the desensitization in the world will not put him fully at ease and able to cope with groups. He will need to be taught these responses and assertive training is a good approach toward reaching this goal. The importance of choosing relevant therapeutic goals is apparent.

Mr. Esterhazy, a 35-year-old college teacher, developed severe anxiety whenever he had to speak in professional gatherings. The anxiety began shortly after he had chaired an alumni meeting at which some prominent, nationally-known political figures were present. The anxiety spread to his lecturing in the classroom and to faculty committee meetings he was required to attend. Discomfort was maximal when he had to take responsibility for presenting material, as in his classroom teaching or in giving a paper at a professional convention. The anxiety was less when he was not "on the spot," such as when a student led a classroom discussion or when he could listen passively in a committee meeting.

He was able to continue working, but with great discomfort and apprehension. Each morning was a trial for him and the anxiety mounted as he approached the building and the room where he taught. Tranquilizers were of little help and after six months of vainly trying to overcome his fear, he came for therapy. There was no evidence of secondary gain being involved in the maintenance of the symptom and systematic desensitization was chosen as the treatment technique for the patient.

In constructing a hierarchy of anxiety-evoking scenes:

About five different scenes would be included ranging from the least anxiety-evoking (such as attendance at a committee meeting) to the most anxiety-evoking (such as lecturing to his class)..........................turn to page 151.

Well over 20 scenes would be included; for example, one general situation such as lecturing in the classroom would be broken down into several smaller constituent scenes..turn to page 149.

Some patients may complain of anxiety in certain situations but a careful evaluation of the problem (often including interviews with other members of the family) reveals an interpersonal etiology of the avoidance behavior. With these patients, many of whom would conventionally be classed as agoraphobics, the predominant motivating force is positive reinforcement for the "phobia" from significant others: For example, a husband may inadvertently (or for reasons of his own psychological economy) respond to his wife's insistence that she cannot go out alone by providing sympathy, devotedness and even his constant presence. The wife's "talk about anxiety" is reinforced by her husband's nurturing companionship. The treatment approach here would be couple therapy aimed at teaching the husband to reinforce more adaptive, independent behavior by the wife, switching the contingencies of reinforcement away from the problem.

You get the point. Constructing many scenes by filling in small graphic details within the context of a general scene, such as Mr. Esterhazy lecturing in a classroom, is necessary (a) to maximize imagery, (b) to facilitate transfer to the real situation outside the office, and (c) to prevent excessively large increments in anxiety between steps in the hierarchy. If the increment of anxiety in one step is too great, relaxation will cease and progress will be blocked.

The actual hierarchy used in Mr. Esterhazy's case was as follows, from least to most anxiety:

1. Listening in a faculty committee meeting.
2. Speaking at a faculty committee meeting.
3. Having a conference with his immediate supervisor;
   a. in his own office,
   b. in his supervisor's office.
4. Having a joint conference with several colleagues collaborating on research.
5. Sitting in on an oral exam for a graduate student.
6. Questioning the graduate student at an oral examination.
7. Presenting his research to a departmental seminar.
8. Presenting his research to an interdisciplinary seminar.
9. Giving a speech at a professional meeting;
   a. preparing the speech,
   b. reviewing his notes the evening before the meeting,
   c. getting ready for the meeting: arising, dressing, breakfast, etc.,
   d. entering the room where the meeting is held,
   e. chatting with acquaintances at the meeting,
   f. waiting his turn to present the speech,
   g. being introduced to speak,
   h. speaking at the meeting (this can be further broken down).
10. Moderating a discussion in his class with a student being responsible for the presentation.
11. Giving a lecture in his class;
   a. preparing the lecture,
   b. reviewing the notes for the lecture the evening before,
   c. getting ready for the lecture: arising, dressing, breakfast, etc.,
   d. driving to school to give the lecture,
   e. entering the building,
   f. climbing the stairs to the classroom,
   g. entering the classroom,
   h. greeting the assembled students,
   i. waiting for the remainder of the students to arrive,
   j. introducing the topic for the lecture and tying it together with what went on previously in the course,
   k. giving the lecture from notes, using the blackboard, asking students questions, answering questions etc.,
   l. finishing the lecture, and dismissing the class.

You would construct an anxiety hierarchy of five different scenes ranging from the least to the most anxiety-evoking. Your general approach is correct, but the work of constructing a hierarchy only begins with the outlines of a few general scenes.

It is necessary to fill in the fine-grain details of these scenes and to break them down into small, stepwise progressions along the anxiety dimension. It is also wise to introduce scenes intervening between the major ones, often along a temporal dimension. For example, we would want to have Mr. Esterhazy imagine himself driving to work, between his picturing himself at home in the morning and later in the classroom. Relaxation is sufficient to counter-condition mild anxiety, but not severe anxiety; thus if the steps in the hierarchy are too great, the anxiety flooding the patient will overcome the relaxation and progress will be nil.

Go back to page 147 and choose the other answer.

Variations of the basic desensitization procedure have been used successfully. Hypnosis can induce relaxation in people who have difficulty relaxing with the standard training. Some therapists believe that the use of subanesthetic doses of a short-acting barbiturate like Brevital is the best way to effect desensitization since the drug causes deeper and faster relaxation and has a primary anti-anxiety action of its own. However, because of the rare allergic responses to barbiturates, this method should be performed in a hospital and is not appropriate for the typical outpatient setting.

Another variation is called "in vivo" desensitization, a technique in which the patient is exposed to the real-life anxiety-evoking situations instead of to the imagined situations. Here, too, a hierarchy is constructed and the therapist guides the patient through it in graded steps. Relaxation can be used in the real-life situations, but frequently the trusting and comforting relationship with the therapist is sufficient to override the anxiety. In vivo desensitization probably accounts for many so-called spontaneous remissions where the person rids himself of a fear by gradually exposing himself to small increments of anxiety in a stepwise fashion. In vivo desensitization has been used with notable effectiveness with agoraphobics—the therapist leads the patient to ever increasing distances from home or hospital maintaining relaxation. In one case, the therapist accompanied a patient on the subway system and within 10 sessions a seven-year fear of tunnels was mastered.

Desensitization can be done in a group of individuals all having a common avoidance problem. A common hierarchy is constructed and the group's progression is paced by the rate of the slowest member. With groups, relaxation or in vivo guidance can be used—with the latter approach, group members can be guides for each other with effectiveness preserved and economy of therapist time achieved.

You should keep in mind that each patient must have a tailor-made hierarchy, even though certain parts of a hierarchy dealing with a frequent problem (e.g., fear of taking exams, fear of social scrutiny) can be used with different individuals. Some frequently used hierarchies are presented in Wolpe and Lazarus' book, *Behavior Therapy Techniques*.

The hierarchy can be added to or modified as the desensitization proceeds, especially if a step has to be broken down into smaller components to deal with particularly extreme anxiety. *Each step is repeated, many times if necessary, until the patient is free of anxiety during its presentation.* Only then can the therapist move on to the next scene in the hierarchy.

In Mr. Esterhazy's case, once the anxiety hierarchy was completed and he mastered deep muscular relaxation, it took a total of eight sessions for him to move through the hierarchy and obtain a complete remission of anxiety. One year later he was still free of anxiety, and functioning well without other symptoms.

SUMMARY OF CHAPTER 9

1. Systematic desensitization is a method useful in the treatment of avoidance problems maintained by anxiety. Phobias are particularly susceptible to this approach.

2. Desensitization of anxiety or fear occurs when the patient learns to substitute deep muscle relaxation for anxiety in the imagined presence of the feared scenes or situations.

3. Relaxation is a response incompatible with the experiencing of anxiety.

4. By systematically presenting a hierarchy of anxiety-evoking scenes (from least to greatest in amount of anxiety) to the patient's imagination while he remains deeply relaxed, anxiety is counter-conditioned.

5. Hierarchies must be individualized to meet the particular needs of each patient.

6. Desensitization can occur with the use of a short-acting barbiturate (Brevital) or hypnosis to induce relaxation as well as by having the patient test the reality of his fears in a stepwise fashion in real-life situations (in vivo desensitization).

7. Some anxiety-based problems require the building up of positive responses other than relaxation (e.g., assertiveness) when there are marked deficits of needed pro-social behavior in the patient's repertoire.

Chapter 10: BEHAVIOR THERAPY WITH NEUROTICS: ASSERTIVE TRAINING

Assertive training consists of a variety of behavioral techniques which have as their goal the facilitation of self-expression by the patient. Assertive training is a valuable therapeutic tool for patients with difficulties in expressing justified resentment and anger or for patients who are passive and withdrawn in interpersonal situations. Some patients are inhibited from being more forceful by the anxiety they experience in social situations which call for assertiveness on their part. They can be helped to master their fear by learning assertive responses, since a person who is expressing his feelings with vigor cannot at the same time feel anxious. In some cases training is desirable to promote expression of anger or irritation. In other cases the expression of such socially-appropriate emotions as pleasure and joy, sadness, affection and intimacy, and saying "no" to unreasonable requests has to be taught. Individuals who can benefit from assertive training may *never* have learned how to show anger or joy or may have been punished for asserting themselves —often in childhood—and hence are conditioned to have anxious or passive responses to interpersonal relationships.

In assertive training the therapist takes a clearly defined educational approach with the patient. The therapist points out the dysfunctional consequences of failure to assert oneself, and instructs the patient, using both hypothetical and real situations, in how to improve his expressions of affect. Instruction proceeds by prompting and encouraging the patient in appropriate self-assertion. The therapist consciously provides himself as a model of reasonable assertiveness, thereby encouraging the patient to imitate or identify with him. The therapist also praises or uses other subtle means of approving the patient's efforts at assertiveness that take place either in the therapy situation itself or outside the therapy session. Of course, the effectiveness of such instruction will depend upon the presence of a collaborative and satisfying therapeutic relationship.

If you have had clinical experience with non-behavioral psychotherapy, you will recognize that some of the work you do with patients really amounts to assertive training. The techniques and goals are not unique to behavior therapy but rather have been imbedded in various successfully-conducted therapies and counseling efforts. Behavior therapists have simply defined the desired goals more explicitly, and have worked toward them more systematic-

ally. Many psychodynamically-oriented therapists encourage their patients to freely express hostility and irritation towards them—really a form of assertive training. A study evaluating the outcome of psychotherapy suggests that learning assertiveness may be an important ingredient for clinical improvement. Storrow and Spanner (1962) found that those patients receiving "short-term, non-intensive psychotherapy who described themselves as more dominant after therapy, also tended to describe themselves as improved."

Another technique used for assertive training is role-playing or behavioral rehearsal. Here the therapist takes either the role of a person with whom the patient in real life is trying to assert himself or takes the role of the patient and demonstrates the desired assertiveness. For example, a teacher was having difficulty responding to criticism by parents who called on the phone. The therapist engaged him in a behavioral rehearsal using one office phone while the teacher used another; they practiced alternate and more assertive responses to the problem situation, switching the teacher and parent roles back and forth.

The therapist and patient can re-create the problematic situation in the safety of the office and try out various interactions until one is encountered that "feels" right to the patient. The situation can be broken down into its parts and gradually built up, using the learning principle of shaping. As the patient successively approximates the desired response, he is given social reinforcement by the therapist in the form of approval and encouragement. Behavioral rehearsal can be used to achieve similar goals in family therapy and group therapy. The effectiveness of psychodrama as a therapeutic method rests on its structuring opportunities for the patient to behave in adaptive ways—the psychodramatist provides social reinforcement for the behavior and the observing patients can imitate the scenario if it is relevant to their own behavioral deficits.

The principles of learning inherent in assertive training are:

A. Extinction of anxiety responses associated with assertive behavior.
B. Punishment of lack of assertiveness.
C. Differential reinforcement for socially appropriate assertiveness.
D. Negative reinforcement of anxiety.
E. Learning assertiveness by limitation.

If all of the above are correct.......................... turn to page 163.
If A, C and E are correct.............................. turn to page 165.
If B and D are correct .... turn to page 167.

You think that assertive training encompasses all of the principles of learning listed on page 161. You are only half right. Maybe the basic principles are not clear enough to you yet. Let's go over the specific meaning of each of the principles listed.

A. Extinction of anxiety responses associated with assertive behavior: The therapist is non-punitive when the patient asserts himself, and anxiety slowly diminishes.

B. Punishment of lack of assertiveness: The therapist applies an aversive stimulus (verbal or physical) to the patient when he fails to assert himself, anxiety is heightened in the therapeutic setting and the patient is less likely to give any response.

C. Differential reinforcement for socially appropriate assertiveness: The therapist approves of behavior that increasingly approximates the desired degree and quality of assertiveness.

D. Negative reinforcement of anxiety: The level of anxiety is increased by the removal of a noxious stimulus whenever anxiety occurs.

E. Learning assertiveness by imitation: The relevant behaviors shown by the therapist are imitated by the patient. This process has also been called identification.

Now do you know which principles apply for assertive training? If you now have chosen principles A, C and E you are correct. If you're still unclear about this, re-read Chapters 3, 5, 6, and 8 in Part I.

Now turn to page 171.

You correctly understand that assertive training precedes by (1) differential positive reinforcement of self-assertion, (2) the extinction of anxiety previously associated with self-assertion, and (3) learning by identifying with (imitating) the therapist's assertiveness.

As you know, the consequences of behavior largely determine its future course. In the case of assertive training, the patient's expression of appropriate feelings are responded to by the therapist with approval and not with repressive measures (which may have been the responses of significant others in the patient's life and hence led to anxiety and the suppression of assertiveness in the first place). With punitive measures no longer following self-assertiveness, the anxiety extinguishes and the positive reinforcement and modeling provided by the therapist shapes successively more adaptive behavior.

For the method to fully succeed, it will be necessary for the patient to experience this same sequence of consequences with people in his milieu. To maximize the probability of assertiveness generalizing to outside situations, the therapist paces the patient's fledgling attempts at assertiveness with deliberateness and instructs the patient not to go beyond the point reached in therapy. To avoid negative consequences outside of therapy, the therapist must define socially appropriate assertiveness carefully and not give positive reinforcement for excessive self-assertion. The goal is for the patient to become assertive without being abrasive.

Now turn to page 171.

You picked statements B and D as describing principles involved in assertive training. While punishment and negative reinforcement are basic principles of learning, they are not operative in assertive training. In fact, the patient with anxiety in situations where he should assert himself has probably developed this anxiety because important people in his past have punished him for attempts at asserting himself. The therapist tries to reverse this process using other means. Punishing the patient for lacking assertiveness leads nowhere except to greater anxiety in the presence of the therapist. Since negatively reinforcing anxiety would only serve to increase anxiety in the future, you would certainly not expect this mechanism inherent in assertive training. Remember that negative reinforcement is defined as the increase of the targeted behavior by the individual being able to escape or avoid aversive consequences. Assertive responses rather than anxiety are negatively reinforced by this procedure because as the patient learns to express himself more forcefully, he can escape and avoid being exploited, humiliated, and deprecated.

Go back to page 161 and pick another answer.

SUMMARY OF CHAPTER 10

1. Assertive training encompasses a range of interpersonal techniques which have as their goal teaching the patient to more effectively express his feelings.

2. Behaving assertively is incompatible with feeling anxious; hence, individuals who have learned to express their anger and affirm their rights and desires no longer experience incapacitating anxiety in social situations.

3. The behavioral principles underlying assertive training are:

   a. Extinction of anxiety responses in social situations.
   b. Differential positive reinforcement for socially appropriate expressions of assertiveness.
   c. Imitation of assertive responses.

Chapter 11: TRADITIONAL VERBAL PSYCHOTHERAPY AS BEHAVIOR THERAPY

The purpose of this section is to familiarize the dynamically-oriented therapist with some behavioral aspects of his own work. Because insight therapy is a learning experience for both patient and therapist, the perceptive therapist is already aware of his potency as a reinforcer or personal influence. Such a therapist can become more conscious and systematic in his responses to patients' behavior in order to catalyze beneficial changes.

It has been said that a therapist changes a patient without influencing him. Let us evaluate this paradox with the following example.

Rhona, a 15-year-old girl, was hospitalized because of running away from home and sexual acting out. After a short "honeymoon period," her behavior in the hospital became obstreperous and difficult to control. She escaped numerous times and taunted the staff by being sexually provocative with male patients. Her therapist used his relationship with her to focus on her lack of self-control, to interpret her sexual misbehavior, and to be non-judgmental and accepting. Her behavior only became worse, to the irritation of the nurses and attendants. She was on the verge of being sent to a more custodial institution when the staff decided to take a different tack with her.

On the one hand, firm limits were provided and any misbehavior led to restrictions on her freedom of movement and other hospital privileges. On the other hand, Rhona's psychiatrist paid considerable attention to her age-appropriate behavior, such as her attending the hospital school, and engaging in supervised and scheduled social activities.

Instead of clarifying the intrapsychic and childhood roots of her behavior, Rhona's doctor kept to the here-and-now by reviewing in detail her daily activities and feelings. He furthermore openly indicated his approval and interest in her tentative involvements in ward activities and her concrete plans for the immediate future. When the contingencies of the doctor's attention switched, Rhona began to improve rapidly and within two months was discharged to her home and school.

Rhona's improvement was a result of:

Her intrinsic drive toward self-actualization which was fostered during the early period of hospitalization when the staff was supportive and accepting........
.... turn to page 177.

The differential response to her maladaptive and adaptive behavior—punishment and positive reinforcement respectively—by her therapist and the ward staff . . . . turn to page 175.

Research conducted by the author highlights the lawfulness of the therapist's influence on the behavior of his patients. The study (Liberman, 1970) was carried out with two outpatient, non-psychotic therapy groups. One therapist was trained to systematically reinforce (through use of such attentional mechanisms as paraphrasing, clarifying, or indicating approval) expressions of cohesiveness by the group members. The comparison group's therapist managed his sessions in a more intuitive fashion along group dynamic lines. The experimental approach led to significantly greater cohesiveness and correlated personality and symptomatic improvements. However, both groups exhibited similar positive relationships between the therapist and the patients, indicating that a therapist will have direct influence on the behavior of his group members even if he is unaware of it.

REINFORCEMENT + PROMPTING COHESIVENESS:
IPA CATEGORIES 1 + 3

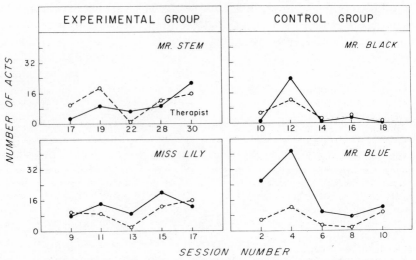

Fig. 6. (From Liberman, R. P. A Behavioral Approach to Group Dynamics. *Behavior Therapy*, 1970, Vol. 1, p. 164. Copyright Academic Press, New York, 1970.)

Figure 6 shows the close correlation between the therapists' prompting and reinforcing cohesiveness and patients' responding in this dimension. The influence of the therapist on the group members appears whether the data come from individual patients as in Fig. 6 or from the group as a whole.

You correctly saw Rhona's improvement as a result of differential application of rewards and punishments to her adjusted and maladaptive behavior. You are able to recognize the functional relationship between behavior and its environmental consequences. When Rhona's misdeeds were rewarded with attention, she was not motivated to change. When it became clear to her that she could gain attention and privileges only by changing, she began immediately to respond to the new contingencies.

This case contributes to our understanding that, for good or ill, our patients will respond to the contingencies we (knowingly or unknowingly) set up. Thus while a certain amount of unconditional regard, empathy, and acceptance solidify a therapeutic relationship, they should not be provided in such a way as to permit the patient's maladaptive behavior to be rewarded. It is clear in Rhona's case that she experienced the staff's permissiveness and warm attentiveness as pay-offs for her misbehavior.

The behavioral view of well-conducted psychotherapy emphasizes two phases of the process. First there must be a positive therapeutic alliance established between the patient and the therapist to enable the latter to function as a social reinforcer. Unless the patient respects and likes the therapist, the therapist will have little influence on the patient's behavior. The second phase of therapy involves the therapist *using* his relationship with the patient in a systematic, contingent fashion to help alter the patient's responses to stimuli. These stimuli can be internal, as for example Rhona's sexual feelings, as well as external such as the presence of male patients and supervisory staff to flaunt. The therapist who thinks behaviorally will consciously use his interest, approval and concern in subtle ways to gradually move the patient toward the therapeutic goals. In choosing specific goals and working toward them consistently using the therapeutic relationship as the lever for change, the behaviorally-oriented therapist differs from his colleague who more conventionally functions in an intuitive and less directive manner.

While Rhona may have had a drive towards self-actualization, it certainly did not show up while the milieu was supportive and totally accepting. In fact, during the time she received unconditional acceptance and toleration from the therapist and the staff, her behavior got worse.

Ferster (1963) has explained the therapeutic failure of a totally accepting environment in the following manner

> If one accepts everything and reacts to all behaviors in the same way, one essentially deprives the person of an opportunity to differentiate between his adaptive and maladaptive behaviors. The person who displays complete tender-loving-care is acting as if what the person is doing made no difference.

Re-read the case study and choose the correct answer.

Extract by Carl R. Rogers, from "Some Issues Concerning the Control of Human Behavior: A Symposium," in *Science*, 1956, **124,** 1057–1066:

In client-centered therapy, we are deeply engaged in the prediction and influencing of behavior, or even the control of behavior. As therapists, we institute certain attitudinal conditions, and the client has relatively little voice in the establishment of these conditions. We predict that if these conditions are instituted, certain behavioral consequences will ensue in the client.*

* Reprinted with permission of the American Association for the Advancement of Science, Washington, D.C., from C. R. Rogers and B. F. Skinner's Some Issues Concerning the Control of Human Behavior: A Symposium, in *Science*, Vol. 124, pp. 1057–1066, 30 November 1956.

An important way that the psychodynamically-oriented therapist facilitates behavior change is through focusing his sympathy, interest, praise and concern on specific behavior performed or talked about by the patient. As the patient talks about his feelings, expresses emotion, gains insight into the historical roots of his problem, the therapist will respond to certain issues more than others. The patient will learn which behaviors will most likely produce a response from his therapist. The therapist's responses—whether in the form of clarification, interpretations, or subtle forms of concern and interest—can reinforce selected behaviors in the patient. The process of reinforcement can lead the patient toward more appropriate expression of feelings or toward insight.

Insight can be described as a form of verbal learning in which the patient is taught to understand and label his behavior according to the way his therapist understands it. Research has shown that patients treated by therapists adhering to different schools of psychotherapy end therapy with insight very much concordant with the theories of their therapist's respective "school" (Heine, 1953). This concordance in terminology derives from the patient imitating his therapist's interpretations and being reinforced by the therapist's explicit and implicit approval.

The patient will sooner or later try out what he has learned in therapy in his real-life environment; if he has learned improved interpersonal coping methods, these will be, in turn, reinforced by others outside of therapy. Particularly gifted therapists will intuitively arrange the sequence of issues worked on in therapy so that the patient can *gradually* adopt new patterns of interaction that will "pay-off" outside of therapy. Such therapists help guard the patient from taking too great a leap into a new behavior pattern since it may produce awkwardness in the patient as he tries out new ways with others. This awkwardness may be even offensive to others, lead to coolness or rejection in the response he gets and hence become a self-defeating cycle. Thus the learning principle of "shaping" plays an important part in successful therapy.

On the path towards incorporating new behavior, a patient may ask himself how his therapist would expect him to behave. This type of verbal rehearsal:

> Utilizes the therapist's expectations learned in therapy as discriminative stimuli and is desirable...............................turn to page 183.

> Is anti-therapeutic since the patient may be led to do things solely to please the therapist and not for himself............................turn to page 185.

Extract by Judd Marmor, from "Theories of Learning and The Psycho-therapeutic Process," in *British J. Psychiatry*, 1966, **112,** 363–366:

What goes on in successful psychotherapy is a unique kind of learning process in which the therapist employs his particular theoretical frame of reference as a rational basis for explaining the patient's past and present difficulties, and by non-verbal as well as verbal cues, uses the instrument of a warm empathic and meaningful human relationship as a means of helping the patient to persist in the difficult task of combating his anxieties, overcoming his resistance, and learning more mature patterns of adaptation . . . the non-verbal as well as verbal reactions of the therapist act as positive and negative reinforcing stimuli to the patient, encouraging certain kinds of responses and discouraging others. What seems to be going on in the working through process is a kind of conditioned learning, in which the therapist's overt or covert approval and disapproval—expressed in his non-verbal reactions as well as in his verbal confrontations, and in what he interprets as neurotic or healthy—act as reward-punishment cues or conditioning stimuli. The analyst's implicit or explicit approval acts as a positive reinforcement to the more "mature" patterns of reacting, while his implicit or explicit disapproval tends to inhibit the less "mature" patterns.

This should not be misunderstood as negating the paramount importance in the therapeutic transaction of the therapist's genuine interest in the patient's welfare, and belief in his fundamental worth as a human being. It may be useful, however, to make a distinction between such basic *acceptance* of the patient and *approval* of his behavior.*

Very good. You remembered from Chapter 7 that a discriminative stimulus marks the time or place of reinforcement being presented or removed. In rehearsing to himself what his therapist might expect of him, the patient is anticipating the imagined approval (reinforcement) he will get (directly in therapy, or vicariously in imagery) from his therapist for doing the "right" or "mature" thing. This process of discrimination learning in which the therapist becomes an internalized discriminative stimulus, is similar to the socialization process in childhood where the parents, peer groups, teachers, and culture heroes take on properties of discriminative stimuli.

Discrimination learning is desirable and we should not fool ourselves by renouncing our role as influencers of behavior. Denial of our role as agents of behavior modification will not cause this role to disappear. A study by Rosenthal (1955) illustrates the salutary effect of communication of values in psychotherapy. Patients who were rated as "improved" changed significantly in the direction of values held by their therapists on a test reflecting the areas of sex, aggression, and authority. On the other hand, "unimproved" patients tended to become less like their therapists in these values.

Awareness and acceptance of his role as an agent of behavior control should lead the psychotherapist not to play "God" but rather to a sensitive and thoughtful respect for the values he is transmitting in the therapeutic process. This requires the therapist to take a large measure of responsibility for collaborating with the patient in formulating and working toward the goals of treatment.

You felt that a patient's silent rehearsal of what his therapist would expect of him is anti-therapeutic, since it would lead the patient to act to please the therapist. Now why is acting in a way that would please a therapist anti-therapeutic? Isn't this the way learning takes place generally? Actions that please the therapist can also be pleasing to the patient, and to his family and friends as well.

The difficulty that you foresee, however, might be a real one. That is the development of an excessively dependent relationship with the therapist. This is indeed a problem to avoid, but it is generated by a different set of contingencies than imagined rehearsal of therapist's expectations. One way to develop dependency is to set up ground rules that prevent the patient from making any important life decisions while he is in therapy. Other ways are to positively reinforce infantile-like behavior, or to endlessly sympathize with the patient's complaints so that he is never ready to terminate, or to structure the therapy so that it takes many years to complete.

Go back to page 181 and read the correct answer.

Freud was very much aware of the processes by which a therapist influences his patient. A proper goal for all therapists, whatever their theoretical persuasions, will be to combine the effective elements underlying various types of therapeutic practice into a group of teachable procedures that can be shown to help particular patients with particular problems. Flexibility and a willingness to change and innovate should be guiding lights for all of us.

In "Further Recommendations on The Technique of Psychoanalysis," *Collected papers*, Vol. 2, pp. 342. London: Hogarth Press, 1948, Freud stated:

> Since while I listen, I resign myself to the control of my unconscious thoughts, I do not wish my expression to give the patient indications which he may interpret or which may influence him in his communications.

And in his "On Psychotherapy," *Collected papers*, Vol. 1, pp. 251–256. New York: Basic Books, 1959, he wrote:

> Is it not then a justifiable endeavor on the part of a physician to seek to control this factor (of expectant faith)—to use it with a purpose, and to direct and strengthen it? This and nothing else is what scientific psychotherapy proposes.
>
> There are many ways and means of practicing psychotherapy. All that lead to recovery are good.
>
> I consider it quite justifiable to resort to more convenient methods of healing as long as there is any prospect of attaining anything by their means. That, after all, is the only point at issue.

Another behavioral feature of psychotherapy is the process of extinction. Anxiety becomes conditioned to behavior that may be adaptive but which has been squelched repeatedly in the past by a parent or others. Some over-protective parents, for example, suppress independent and assertive behavior in their children using discipline or guilt mechanisms that last into adolescence and even beyond. If the therapist does not give the aversive responses to this behavior expected from a parent-surrogate, the anxiety conditioned to it will eventually extinguish. This depends upon the patient viewing the therapist on some level as being similar to the parent(s) (transference). Gradually, the formerly suppressed behavior will enter the patient's repertoire where it can be positively reinforced by the therapist and others. This effect frequently enables a patient to improve his self-assertive or aggressive responses and gives him the good-feelings and sense of accomplishment that develop in therapy.

Another way that therapeutic extinction occurs is when the therapist does not respond to or reinforce maladaptive or provocative behavior displayed by the patient. The maladaptive behavior will gradually dissipate allowing the patient to emit other, more adaptive behavior which will more successfully engage the therapist's interest and responsiveness. If the principle of extinction is used systematically and consciously by the therapist, it can be a valuable therapeutic tool.

Steve was a 21-year-old hippie who came to see the psychiatrist initially to obtain an evaluation for his draft board. A strong, positive relationship developed rapidly and he decided to continue in therapy. The therapist, from the start, almost completely ignored Steve's provocative talk about his use of marijuana and LSD. On the other hand, whenever Steve spoke about his efforts in constructive activity—such as taking a university extension course—the therapist showed intense interest and responsiveness. Within three months, Steve's use of drugs tailed off markedly and he was making plans to return to college on a full-time basis.

Mrs. Prior had been in psychotherapy for six months. She came complaining of depression and feelings of worthlessness and spent most of each session castigating herself for her deficiencies as a wife and mother. Initially her therapist listened with interest and empathic understanding, but soon became bored and annoyed with Mrs. Prior's self-flailing and remonstrations of helplessness. The therapist decided to ignore her self-deprecations and instead to show active interest whenever she spoke of doing something constructive. Soon, Mrs. Prior's depressive talk decreased and she spent more and more of the therapy sessions describing her homemaking and child-rearing efforts at home. The relating of more adaptive behavior was greeted by pleasure and encouragement by the therapist.

The therapist's initial response to Mrs. Prior was:

To positively reinforce her negative feelings about herself......turn to page 191.

To positively reinforce her sense of self-esteem.............. turn to page 193.

You chose the first statement and you are correct. Interest and understanding from a therapist can be a powerful means of positive reinforcement which can function inadvertently to increase the frequency of maladaptive behavior. While a certain amount of unconditional warmth, acceptance and empathy is necessary in the early stages of *any* therapy, including behavior therapy, to cement a positive relationship and hence enhance the positively reinforcing value of the therapist's responses, it may backfire when directed too long at the patient's psychopathology.

During the later stages of therapy with Mrs. Prior, the therapist:

Extinguished Mrs. Prior's self-disparaging remarks and began to positively reinforce her describing her adaptive efforts . . . . turn to page 195.

Negatively reinforced Mrs. Prior's self-disparaging remarks and began to positively reinforce her describing her adaptive efforts . . . . turn to page 197.

You said that the therapist was positively reinforcing Mrs. Prior's sense of self-esteem. That would be true if Mrs. Prior were happy with her deficiencies. In fact, she wants and needs to be able to overcome her helplessness. Therefore her self-esteem will be more likely to improve if attention is paid to self-help rather than to helpless behavior.

During the later stages of therapy with Mrs. Prior, the therapist:

Extinguished Mrs. Prior's self-disparaging remarks and began to positively reinforce her describing her adaptive efforts .... turn to page 195.

Negatively reinforced Mrs. Prior's self-disparaging remarks and began to positively reinforce her describing her adaptive efforts......turn to page 197.

Efforts are in progress to systematically exploit principles of reinforcement in the treatment of depressed patients. Lewinsohn and his colleagues (1969) are capitalizing on the observation that depressed patients tend to spend much time complaining about their psychological and somatic discomfort. Using the Premack Principle (*see* Chapter 3), they have structured therapy sessions so that in order to engage in "depressive talk," the patient must first spend time talking about more positive feelings and behaviors. Making high frequency depressive talk contingent upon engaging in low frequency adaptive talk raises the rate of the latter, while bringing under the therapist's control the amount of time spent on the former. Their patients report rapid resolution of symptoms and an enhanced feeling of being able to control their emotions.

You said that the therapist, during the later stages of therapy, extinguished Mrs. Prior's self-deprecations and began to positively reinforce her talking about her adaptive activities. You are right on the track to an understanding of the functional relationship between the patient and the patient's therapeutic environment—the social reinforcement emanating from her therapist. Since Mrs. Prior values the concern and interest of her therapist, she will tend to relate thoughts, feelings, and actions that enlist the therapist's attention. The ability of the therapist to influence the content of the patient's talk and indirectly the patient's behavior outside of therapy is the cornerstone of all verbal psychotherapies.

While generalization of behavior change from the therapy context to the real-world outside can be a problem, in Mrs. Prior's case the depression rapidly lifted and she terminated therapy within one month of her therapist's changing the contingencies.

Sorry, I haven't made the concept of "negative reinforcement" clear enough. Negative reinforcement is frequently misused in the vernacular and confused with extinction or punishment. Negative reinforcement occurs when by performing some act to avoid or escape an aversive stimulus, an individual then has a higher probability of repeating that act in the future. Take another look at the section in Chapter 3 that describes negative reinforcement.

You are right about the second part of the statement—the therapist does indeed begin to positively reinforce Mrs. Prior's discussing her adaptive efforts at home. We would hope that this redirection of social reinforcement will indirectly increase her adaptive efforts at home—that the in-therapy verbal conditioning will generalize to the really important, extra-therapy behavior. While generalization of behavior change can be a problem, in Mrs. Prior's case the depression rapidly lifted and she terminated therapy within one month of her therapist's changing the contingencies.

A third behavioral approach found in psychodynamic therapies is the use of modeling or imitation. This is the same as the process called identification or incorporation by psychoanalytic writers. Much clinical material has been written on this topic, but therapists have failed to develop explicit and systematic methods through which learning by imitation or identification can take place. This is an area for future exploration.

Already a psychologist who has done much basic research in the area of modeling, Bandura (1969), has published several accounts of specific clinical applications of this process. In one project, children who were afraid of dogs were exposed to the model of a peer who exhibited progressively stronger approach responses toward a dog. These children later showed stable and generalized reduction of their fears and differed significantly in this respect from children in various control groups. Bandura's work replicates the study of Mary Cover Jones (1924) who over 40 years ago extinguished children's phobic responses to animals by having them observe their peers play with the animals in a pleasurable manner. A recent study by Friedman (1970) showed that modeling together with role-playing was the most effective treatment for inducing college students to become more assertive.

Extract from C. B. Ferster and Jeanne Simons' "Behavior Therapy with Children," *Psychological Record*, 1966, **16,** 65–71.

To the extent that it is successful, much conventional therapy is behavior therapy. Some of the apparent difference between the activity of clinicians and behavior therapists comes from the frequent use of food (or relaxation, tokens, or shock) as a reinforcer in behavior therapy. Whenever we have observed successful clinicians at work, we have seen them change verbal and nonverbal behavior and manipulate the environment, much as in behavior therapy. The potential contribution of behavior therapy comes when natural science principles are self-consciously applied to clinical problems. With such an approach, the objective and functional description of the environment makes it possible to describe what particular aspects of a complex interaction are having what particular effects on the patient. Hence new procedures can be developed, and old ones refined and their application intensified. With such a natural science philosophy of human nature, the behavior of the therapist is constantly shaped differentially and reinforced by the effect on the patient.*

To summarize, psychodynamic therapies incorporate learning techniques such as conditioning, extinction, and modeling. The difference between traditional and behavior therapies is that the latter uses these techniques and others systematically and explicitly to achieve a behavioral goal defined at the beginning of treatment.

> Any therapeutic procedure carried on without reference to the elements that are really active in it (in the case of psychotherapy the contingencies between patient behavior and therapist response) is at best inefficient and at worst magical. The traditional therapist does influence his patients and we think that he should do so consciously and systematically. If he thinks that there is a particular behavior that will help the patient, he should legitimately do everything in his power to maximize the frequency of that behavior (Ullmann & Krasner, 1965).

Understanding the principles discussed in this chapter is a start in that direction and the use of behavior therapy methods, sometimes in conjunction with an ongoing course of psychodynamic, insight-oriented therapy, would be a further step toward increasing the effectiveness of our work.

Family and couple therapy provide an excellent opportunity for the use of behavioral techniques. The major reinforcers in an individual's life space are members of his family with whom he interacts each day. In recent years, behaviorally-oriented therapists have turned to working with families and couples to maximize the chances for meaningful and enduring behavior modification. Often, the modification of the responses that family members make to the designated patient are the crucial change needed to produce therapeutic results. The Appendix to this book contains an article written by the author which describes some behavioral approaches to family and couple therapy.

Another approach is contingency contracting, wherein each member of a family or couple exchange responsibilities for privileges. For an adolescent in conflict with his parents, the exchange may be performing chores or homework in exchange for time out at night or an allowance. Bonuses are written into contract to reward consistent compliance with the terms of the contract. Thus, a boy who performs all his agreed upon chores for a week may get, as a bonus, an extra late curfew on a weekend night. Penalties or sanctions are also specified to discourage infractions of the contract. It is important to write fair and honest contracts and to have all members of the family sign it, together with the therapist.

SUMMARY OF CHAPTER 11

1. Psychodynamic psychotherapies are learning situations in which the patient is being influenced to change by the therapist.

2. The positive therapeutic alliance or relationship enables the therapist to serve as a social reinforcer for the patient.

3. Using attention, interest, acknowledgement and interpretation, the therapist can differentially reinforce certain behaviors and verbalizations and extinguish others.

4. The therapist also acts as a behavioral model for the patient to imitate (identification).

5. Systematic and planned use of principles of learning can increase the effectiveness and efficiency of therapists using psychodynamic, non-directive and other verbal therapies.

Chapter 12: BEHAVIOR THERAPY IN INSTITUTIONS: THE TOKEN ECONOMY

The most neglected of institutionalized patients—chronic, backward psychotics, retardates, and juvenile delinquents—have been receiving behavior therapy in an experimental milieu called the "token economy." The essence of the procedure is the use of tokens (poker chips, credit card blanks, points), which are given to patients as reinforcers for improvements in their personal, social, and occupational behavior. The tokens are exchangeable for goods, services and privileges that the patients value.

The token economy is a microcosm of society outside the institution. The therapeutic environment is structured to show the direct relationship between work and reward, striving and success. It is an environment specially engineered to teach the apathetic institutionalized patient what healthy adaptive people have learned and taken for granted since childhood—that to have food and comforts and to enjoy the privileges of society, one must achieve them through competence in work, personal appearance, and social interaction. The backward patient has traditionally lived in a welfare society where he was paid off for passivity, docility, and apathy—his needs and comforts were provided for unconditionally, no matter whether his behavior was adaptive or bizarre. The token economy sets out to reverse this process, by making the patient responsible for achieving the rewards of his therapeutic environment. The exchangeable relation between tokens and goods, services, and desired activities imbue the tokens with reinforcing value. Patients who formerly had free access to candy, cigarettes, visits to a psychiatrist or other privileges now must pay to obtain them.

The hospital thus becomes more like the real world where work must be performed in order to afford pleasures. For professionals, the reinforcers may be articles published, salaries and bonuses, or a vacation. For chronic patients, the reinforcers are likely to be candy, cigarettes, unusually pleasant sleeping and eating settings, TV, visits with a psychiatrist or a nurse, or weekend passes. The selection of reinforcers is broad enough so that there's something for everybody.

One way of choosing the appropriate reinforcer for a patient is to use a learning principle enunciated by Premack (1959) and applied to patients by Ayllon and Azrin (1968). Any behavior that is preferred or frequently engaged in by a person can be used as a reinforcer for other less preferred or frequent behavior. Following this principle, some chronic patients have worked on a hospital job to get tokens which were then exchanged for the chance to spend 30 minutes sitting in a favored chair. One patient spent long hours feeding birds and squirrels on the hospital grounds (his high frequency behavior). He was subsequently permitted to do this only if he earned tokens by keeping his clothes neat and talking at the group meetings (his low frequency behavior).

Some token economies make entry into the dining hall contingent upon a certain number of tokens; here the primary reinforcing effect of food becomes part of the economic system. Rarely does a patient miss more than one meal before earning the necessary tokens for the dining room. There are so many easy and quick ways to earn tokens that a patient coming to the dining hall "broke" can obtain the necessary tokens in a matter of minutes. As a patient becomes proficient in earning tokens the behavioral requirements for reinforcement are raised. In this stepwise fashion, progressive improvement is sustained.

Patients can earn tokens in a variety of ways, but the critical principle is that the receipt of tokens be made contingent upon some social, personal, or work improvement. Most token systems tailor their programs to individually fit each patient's level of behavior. The particular behavioral deficits or excesses of a patient are carefully delineated and a list is made of the behavioral goals—these are the specific behaviors the patient should be performing if he is to be considered more normal, adaptive, or better functioning. The behavioral goals may fall in various areas—personal grooming, social inter-action, education, or work. Examples of goals selected for individuals are performing a ward job such as cleaning a bathroom sink, tying one's shoe-laces, refraining from talking to oneself in public, completing a sewing task in occupational therapy, appropriate use of cosmetics, and making suggestions at a ward meeting.

It is important that the staff be tuned in to each patient's own baseline level of behavior and reward tiny increments of performance with tokens. Shaping, the giving of rewards for successive approximations to the desired goal, plays an important part in token economies. If a patient has not shaved himself for many years, the staff does not wait for him to do the whole job before giving a token, but instead rewards any approximation toward shaving, such as pick-ing up a razor, or showing interest in other patients shaving.

Successive steps over a period of days might be (1) shaving one stroke after having his face lathered by an attendant, (2) shaving additional strokes until the entire face is clean, (3) lathering his face as well as shaving cleanly, (4) putting the blade in the razor as well as lathering and shaving. Each step along the way to the final goal is rewarded immediately with a token.

Simultaneous with giving a token, the nurse or aide gives approval in the form of verbal statements ("Good," or "That's fine," or "You're doing better now") and non-verbal expressions (smiles, nods). Approval or social reinforcement when paired with the token reinforcement enhances the effect and also prepares the patient for the time when tokens are discontinued and his behavioral progress is maintained by the natural reinforcers around him.

Later, after the patient has learned the value of the tokens and after his repertoire has been enlarged, improvements in his behavior can be rewarded after some time has elapsed—in some systems, the patients are given their tokens on a weekly basis, as if they were on a salary. Some token economies have a "credit card" group which patients can join after reaching a high level of functioning. Patients in this group do not receive tokens but are allowed free access to privileges and goods as long as they maintain their adjustment.

The following list of behavioral goals for a patient residing on a token economy is paired with a schedule of token reinforcement.

TOKEN ECONOMY WEEKLY GOALS FORM

PATIENT Jim M.

SPECIFICS: Based on the Previous Week's Assessment and Suggested New Goals. These Are the Behavior Changes that Seem Like they Can be Realistically Achieved in the Coming Week.   DATE 12-6-71

Item	*Token Amount & Schedule*
1. Bed Made (smooth & neat), Room cleaned (Swept & mopped) clothes picked up—numerous prompts	1. 2 tokens if all completed by 0700.
2. Wash hands & Face, Brush teeth, clean Shave, Hair combed—numerous prompts	2. 3 tokens if completed by 0900. Praise all behaviors
3. Sweep & mop Dayhall in early afternoon—no prompts	3. 3 tokens if completed by 1300, 1 token if after 1300
4. Shower daily—1 prompt	4. 1 token at completion

ASSESSMENT: Enumerate the Changes Actually Obtained for Each of the Above Behaviors At the Week's End. Therapists on Other Shifts Should Make Relevant Notations. THERAPIST V. B./E. R./C. H./E. M.

		TU	W	TH	F	S	S	M
1.	Doing well, might be able to fade	2 tkns	2	2	0	2	2	2
2.	Has difficulty completing these by 0900. Not interested	3	0	0	0	3	3	3
3.	No problems	3	3	3	3	3	3	3
4.	Does well, may fade prompts	1	1	1	1	1	1	1

SUGGESTED NEW GOALS: Based on Your Assessment, Suggest New Goals and Token Amount and Schedule.

1. Continue as above but prompt only twice.	1. Same as above.
2. Continue with same behaviors.	2. Increase to 5 tokens.
3. Continue as above.	3. Decrease to 1 token.
4. Continue as above but do not prompt.	4. Same as above.

5. NOTE: The token increase in #2 & decrease in #3 should keep patient spending in balance but provide greater reinforcement for the less motivated behaviors.

The original of this Completed Form is to be put in Dr. Patterson's Mailbox By Monday Morning. The Duplicate Stays in the Patient's Notebook.   fjn 9-30-71

At the Clinical Research Unit of Camarillo State Hospital, where this patient was treated, the nursing staff updates the token economy for each patient every two weeks. This regular revision promotes constant change and improvement in an individualized manner.

Mr. Green, a chronic schizophrenic, has been hospitalized for fifteen years. He spends almost all his time watching TV in the ward's day room. His personal appearance is disheveled with his shoes untied, his shirt hanging out, his hands and face dirty, and his hair uncombed. He is transferred to a ward where active treatment principles are emphasized in a total-push effort for rehabilitation. The staff members are eager to work with him.

Which of the following approaches will likely succeed in improving his personal grooming?

A. Make access to the TV contingent upon Mr. Green tying his shoes during the first week and then gradually add other improvements in his appearance as pre-conditions for watching TV.

B. Put a meter on the TV which turns on the TV when a token is put in a slot. Make access to the TV room contingent upon placing a token in a turnstile at the door. Then pay Mr. Green tokens for tying his shoes, washing his face and hands, combing his hair, and tucking in his shirt.

C. Give Mr. Green plenty of tender-loving-care and indicate to him that he is a valued member of the unit no matter how he looks.

D. Assign one of the nurses to frequently remind Mr. Green to tie his shoes, wash his face and hands, comb his hair, and tuck in his shirt.

A and B will likely succeed .... turn to page 215.

C and D will likely succeed .... turn to page 219.

All will likely succeed................................turn to page 217.

To be effective, a token program must precisely specify the behaviors to be rewarded. Selective reinforcement of desired behavior can occur only if the staff, who are the dispensers of tokens, can be in common agreement on what behavior is to be reinforced. A good example is the following description of one of the earliest and most successful token economies, still ongoing at Patton State Hospital in California, from O. L. Gericke's "Practical Use of Operant Conditioning Procedures in a Mental Hospital," in *Psychiatric Studies and Projects* (American Psychiatric Assoc., Vol. III, No. 5, June 1965):

> We drew up a list of the desirable behaviors that we expected to influence through the reinforcers. We required each member of the nursing staff to make up his list. One of the behaviors listed was "maintaining personal hygiene." The staff quickly grasped that such a global statement of a goal is of little value to the behavioral engineer. Personal hygiene means many things to many people. We demonstrated that to make this term meaningful we must be more specific. For "personal hygiene" we arrived at the following list: (a) no desquamatus between the toes, (b) no dirt on the instep or heels of the feet, (c) no dirt on legs and knees, (d) no evidence of body odor, (e) no residue in the navel, (f) clean hands and fingernails, (g) neat and recent shave for men, (h) nicely combed hair, and (i) a daily change of underwear. A separate list for the women included appropriate use of cosmetics. It became overwhelmingly evident that although there might be disagreement about poorly defined global goals, the items on the detailed list could be agreed upon without much difficulty and, most important for our purposes, could be selectively reinforced.*

* Reprinted with permission of the author and the American Psychiatric Association, from O. L. Gericke's Practical Use of Operant Conditioning Procedures in a Mental Hospital, in *Psychiatric Studies and Projects*, Vol. III, No. 5, June 1965. Copyright © 1965 by the American Psychiatric Association.

You chose approaches A and B as ones likely to succeed with Mr. Green. Good. You'll make a fine behavioral clinician. It's clear that you've assimilated the principles of contingency management—specifying the behavioral goals, and defining the reinforcer (by Premack's principle). Watching TV is a high frequency behavior for Mr. Green and hence can be used in a contingent fashion to strengthen other, less frequent behaviors. This can be done in a token economy (as in B), but also in a less systematized context so long as the contingency principle is used.

Turn to the bottom of page 219 if you want another example of contingency management. If you feel confident of your grasp of this principle, turn to page 225.

You're not discriminating if you said that all of the approaches will likely succeed. As a behavioral engineer you're batting only 50% and that's no better than chance. Even the Hawthorne Effect, which is that any kind of focusing attention on a person will improve performance, can't make up for the real differences in these approaches. Let's clarify the differences.

Approaches A and B will work because you are making low frequency behavior, good grooming, contingent upon high frequency or preferred behavior—TV watching. Watching TV serves as a reinforcer, either directly in A or mediated by tokens in B, for improvements in personal appearance.

Approaches C and D will probably backfire for reasons cited on page 219.

Turn to page 219.

In choosing approaches C and D you will more likely maintain and even strengthen Mr. Green's sloppiness. You will be giving him attention and interest for and hence reinforce the very behavior you wish to eliminate. All too often this is what happens when tender-hearted staff members try to be "giving" to patients. Let's try another example.

Jane Moore is a ten-year-old retarded girl who spends hours at a time playing with a favorite doll. She rarely interacts with other children in conversation or game-playing, preferring isolated activities with toys. On a token economy her social interaction would be increased by:

Giving her tokens for showing approach behavior toward other children and requiring her to pay tokens for access to her favorite doll .... turn to page 221.

Fining her tokens whenever she spends more than ten minutes in isolated play .... turn to page 223.

You decided that by giving Jane tokens for approaching other children and by making her pay tokens to play with her favorite doll, her deficits in social interaction could be remedied. Now you're on the right track. By placing a contingency on her preferred behavior (doll playing), you are exploiting its value as a reinforcer for infrequent behavior (peer interaction).

Remember, however, not to expect too much too soon from Jane in the way of relating to other children. The task is to shape her social interaction by reinforcing successive approximations to the desired goal. At first, it will be necessary to give her tokens for any sign of interest in other children. When she begins to show frequent attention, you then raise the criterion for reinforcement one step by requiring her to show more sustained attention or to make initial contact with another child, verbally or physically. Later, after this level of interaction has been maintained for a while, you would demand a further increment of social performance before reinforcing her with a token. In this stepwise fashion, she can continue to mature in social competence to whatever will be her full potential.

While the tokens, exchangeable for already established rewards and preferences, can introduce Jane to social behavior, once she begins to interact with other children more natural reinforcers will take over the maintenance and further refinement of her behavior—the social reinforcement she gets from the other children as well as from adults, the kinds of games she will now be able to play in groups, the new places she will discover in group outings, and the pleasure she will obtain from her own active reaching-out toward others.

You said that by assessing Jane a fine whenever she spends more than ten minutes in isolated play, she would be motivated to play with other children. While punishment such as this will suppress the behavior it is contingent on, it is likely to have little enduring effect. In the first place, punishment produces unwanted emotional side-effects and we might expect Jane to exhibit tantrums or other untoward emotionality when she is fined. Secondly, punished behavior is suppressed only temporarily in the presence of the punishing stimulus or person. Jane will resume her withdrawn behavior as soon as her "policeman" leaves the field. But most important is the failure of "punishment alone" strategy to build new, adaptive behavior. Punishment of unwanted behavior in combination with reinforcement of alternate, incompatible and adaptive behavior can be quite effective. But punishing a child with an impoverished behavioral repertoire to begin with is like trying to wring water from a stone.

There is no substitute for the painstaking process of building new behavior from simple units, either by reinforcement or imitation.

Go back to page 219 and choose the correct answer.

A novel way of reinforcing the staff on a behavior modification unit has been devised at the Center for the Study of Behavioral Disorders at Camarillo State Hospital. A biweekly newsletter, containing brief synopses of patients' progress, is distributed to the entire nursing staff. Examples of entries in this newsletter, titled "Journal of the Behavior Mod Squad" are given here:

CRU CREW NEWS
(Vol. I, No. 16, July 30, 1971)

H. B. has remained delusional at a low frequency. However, he has not been free of delusions enough to progress toward earning his staffing. He has appeared in new clothing which is of his own selection and which is much more appropriate.

J. F. remains about the same as last week. We have clearly demonstrated that the bedtime contingencies are effective, but not completely.

J. G. began aversive conditioning for *all* body tics on Tuesday of this week. Under these conditions, he seems to be more calm and composed and under better control of ticking, (Ticquing?). The ability of aversive conditioning to influence ticquing (ticking) was dramatically demonstrated by comparing frequency of all body tics with and without apparatus connected: No. of tics with apparatus—41 per half-hour session; No. of tics without apparatus—63 per 3-minute observation period.

B. H., F. B., and W. P. (the "mumbler's" group) took part in a 60-day follow-up to study the long-term effects of the training for increased speech volume. B. H., who has remained on our unit has maintained an acceptable level of speech volume (8.0 on our arbitrary scale). However, F. B. and W. P. have decreased to a lower level (5.5). It should be noted that the level of all, including those who decreased, is still far above the original level (1.0) which was not distinguishable from room noise as electronically measured. These data in-

dicate that it is necessary to maintain such patients in a stimulating environment to keep the gains made intact. I, R. P., wish to give myself reinforcement by announcing that I have finished a first draft of a paper on this. It is now up to the second author, J. T., to proceed.

M. L. has greatly increased her output of office work. As a result she is earning more tokens. She has another successful weekend at home with her mother. Her mother paid her tokens for doing some tasks in the home which were agreed upon beforehand, but the mother reported that M. also helped with other tasks. This week, the "homework assignments" included her going to the beauty parlor and going to church as a form of social activity. M. and her mother agreed to these. This may turn out to be one of the most successful cases.

A. M. completes treatment next week. He is going on a camping trip for a week, then discharge will be finalized.

M. M. (female) has started a new program this week. She is presently in the baseline phase. She is asked questions concerning her identity and background three times daily. At the present time she is given her tokens (18) daily; but during treatment (contingent phase) she will have to earn her tokens by answering these questions realistically. This one will be fun.

M. M. (male) is showing the results of his program to control tantrums. During

The most important element in the success of token reinforcement programs is the effective involvement of the staff members who act as dispensers of tokens—primarily the nurses and attendants. In most mental hospitals the nurses and attendants develop a custodial approach to patients which combines tender-loving-care and strong-arm methods in the service of keeping the patients compliant and under control. The usual result is the passive, helpless, quiet and docile patient who causes little trouble for the overburdened staff but who has little active behavior in his repertoire. The initial task, then, for the behavioral innovator is to educate the nurses and attendants in a new approach to patient care. The fate of his program will depend entirely upon his success in this re-education effort.

The staff must be taught basic principles of reinforcement, particularly the importance of responding to specific behaviors of each patient in a contingent fashion. Rather than being permitted to provide service and rewards, indiscriminantly, the nurses and aides are taught the importance of selectively rewarding desired behavior in the areas of personal grooming, social interaction, and work. They are taught how to shape new behavior by the method of successive approximations and by modeling. Instead of relying on ritualized orders from above, the nurses and attendants are given direct responsibility for treatment. They collaborate with the project director in specifying the behavioral goals or prescriptions for each patient.

In setting up a token economy, the ward nurses and aides must be:

Selected for their experience and competence in mental hospital work........
....turn to page 229.

Reinforced for their appropriate reinforcement of the patients.............
....turn to page 227.

seven days of baseline, the average two per day. Since treatment began, he averaged less than one per day.

B. S. started a new program recently. Thus far, there appears to be a small decrease in handwriting, but no change in reports of visions.

C. S. has shown a considerable decrease in her "pesky" behavior and is making considerable progress toward earning her "graduation." Notably, she has stopped asking R. F. "when am I getting out of this damn place?" So I asked *her* that question and she told me about her grading and wall chart.

J. W. has shown no increase in delusional talk since her medication was d.c.'d. This one fooled us all. Most of us didn't think that the behavioral treatment alone would be this effective, but she has been rational on her observations and interviews 172 out of the 176 times that measurements have been made since the medication was stoppe⁴.

M. W. (our A.W.O.L.) has returned from S. F., but he didn't make it to the hospital. He just called from his mother's house in L. A. and will be back tomorrow(?).

The newsletter serves as an informational feedback mechanism that maintains staff involvement and morale on a behavior therapy unit. A fuller description of this newsletter is given in *Behavior Therapy*, 1972 ("Reinforcing the reinforcers: A method of supplying feedback to nursing personnel", R. Patterson, C. Cooke and R. Liberman).

You chose the second answer and you are right. Reinforcing the reinforcers is perhaps the most crucial element in the development and maintenance of staff effectiveness in carrying out a token program. Reinforcement for the staff comes from two major sources—the project director and the improvement in the patients.

During the training period and afterwards, it is essential that the project director establish close relationships with nurses and aides. When these relationships are suffused with congeniality, warmth, trust, and mutual respect, the project director's approving comments and positive feedback serve to motivate the staff to keep up the good work. To maintain a successful working relationship it is necessary for the project director to keep in close contact with the ward—being in touch with day-to-day problems, giving assistance to staff, ironing out "bugs" in the program, and providing administrative leadership.

The other source of positive reinforcement for the staff comes from the progress made by the patients in the token system. Generally each nurse or aide is assigned a small group of patients to work with personally. As the behavioral goals are defined and shaping and contingency management begun, the staff member can see salutary changes in the patient's behavior. Although these changes are apparent by simple inspection, it is additionally reinforcing to provide the staff with a notation or data system whereby the daily behavioral progress of the patients can be charted. Charting or graphing the target behaviors, as well as the book-keeping of tokens given out, serves as an indicator of success to the staff person and also is a way to sensitize the staff to the needs for upgrading the program for a particular patient when progress ceases.

Reports from two ongoing token economies illustrate the way nurses and aides are reinforced for their use of behavioral techniques with patients. The first is from James R. Lent's "Mimosa cottage: Experiment in hope" in *Psychology Today*, 1968, **2**, 51–58.

> Isn't it hard for aides to act natural, spontaneous and "happy" with the children when so much behavior is prescribed? When aides first start reinforcing on a schedule, their behavior is somewhat mechanistic and stilted. However, they soon become accustomed to giving reinforcement and they are, after all, pleased when a child behaves appropriately. As the training takes effect, the children behave appropriately more and more often, which reinforces the staff and makes them "happy." The children, in turn, are reinforced by the quiet, predictable, pleasant behavior of the adults in charge.

The second report is by James T. Shelton, M.D., Superintendent, Porterville State Hospital (California) in "The use of operant conditioning with disturbed adolescent, retarded boys" (Paper delivered at 20th Mental Hospital Institute, Washington, D.C., October, 1968):

> One indication of the benefits of efforts put into staff training and development is the comparatively small number of psychiatric technicians who have left the project. Five out of 22 have left, in comparison with a more than 50% turnover in other programs. Reinforcement for the staff came not only from the patient's progress but also from the greater than usual responsibilities they have in the patient's treatment program.

You said that staff members should be selected for a token economy who have experience and competence in mental hospital work. Although this may be desirable, it is not necessary and may in fact be a disadvantage.

Nurses and aides who have years of work behind them on either custodial or active treatment wards have generally learned to pay attention to (reinforce) maladaptive behavior. Their efforts have been focused on controlling deviant behavior after it has been expressed. In this manner, the consequences of the undesirable behavior can paradoxically reinforce it.

Whether the methods of control have been punitive (seclusion, restrictions, drugs or verbal reprimand) or psychotherapeutic (extra time spent talking or sitting with a disturbed patient), frequently the outcome is an increase in the very behavior which the staff would like to control. The attention the patient gets for "sick" behavior becomes valued, especially when there is little staff time to go around.

In a token economy, the nurse or aide must reverse the old process; he must learn to dispense tokens and attention contingent upon desired behaviors and to ignore, for the most part, maladaptive behavior (extinction). Further, the staff members are expected to take a more active and responsible role in treatment than they do in more conventional custodial settings. For instance, they are involved in the formulation of behavioral goals and deciding on-the-spot timing of reinforcements.

Return to page 225 and choose the correct answer.

A general aim of most token economies is to go beyond the improvement of in-hospital behavior to the rehabilitation of the patient for life outside the hospital. This is an ambitious goal for those working with the most chronic and impoverished of psychiatric patients—schizophrenics, retardates, delinquents, and autistic children. To fulfill this goal it becomes necessary to use the learning principle of *generalization* in structuring the environment of the clinical unit.

In the first place, the behaviors targeted for reinforcement should have carry-over value to the community. The behaviors taught the patient should be defined by their utility and appropriateness for the patient when he leaves the unit and goes home or to a job. A knowledge of the cultural variants of acceptable behavior in the community at large is necessary for the behavioral engineer. Patients should be taught behaviors which are not usually found in a large mental hospital—behaviors such as riding a bus, cooking a meal, laundering and ironing clothes, making a telephone call, using a bank, shopping in a supermarket.

In working with chronic schizophrenics and retardates, the clinician cannot take for granted the patient's ability to generalize behavior learned on the ward to the community outside. This means that the training program must explicitly tailor the behavioral goals to fit the demands and expectations which will be placed on the patient when he is discharged and returns to home, job, and community milieu. Leisure time activities, the kinds of behaviors people occupy their time with in the community such as card-playing, bowling, and attendance at theatres and athletic events, should be programmed in a token system. Appropriate sexual behavior must also be taught.

In a token economy for retarded young women, the patients were taught how to recognize stewed tomatoes in a single kind of can and to identify prices marked in a particular way. Later, when some of the women left the hospital to live in the community they had great difficulty choosing canned foods in the supermarket. Their problem in stimulus generalization might have been prevented if prior to discharge:

A. They had been exposed to many different kinds of canned foods and many different pricing systems with specific learning of each on the ward.

B. They had been brought to a local supermarket and taught the varieties of canned foods and pricing systems.

C. Their relatives or foster families had been instructed in reinforcement methods and then, in turn, taught the former patients how to select canned foods in the supermarket.

If A and B are good solutions .... turn to page 235.

If A, B, and C are all good solutions .... turn to page 237.

In choosing answers A and B you indicate that perhaps only the ward staff can learn reinforcement techniques and become effective behavioral engineers. This is not so.

It takes no special professional qualities to master the basic principles of delivering reinforcement in a contingent manner for desired behavior. College students have been quickly taught principles of reinforcement and have then effectively modified behavior of chronic psychotics in hospitals. Parents of autistic children have taken courses in behavior modification and have then successfully worked with their own children. And as we will see in a later section, teachers have learned how to systematically and selectively dispense reinforcement to their pupils to establish studying behavior and to extinguish disruptive behavior.

Turn now to page 237.

Here is a treatment memo sent to the nursing staff at the Clinical Research Unit of Camarillo State Hospital regarding a new patient who is apathetic and inactive.

PROGRAM SUMMARY—CAROL S.

Carol is to start her morning assignments as set up by Bill Moon at 0800. If she completes her first one-hour assignment by 0900 or before, she gets one token and 1 point on the report card. If she has not been pesky (as defined by a memo dated 7/20), she gets a 5-minute conversation, a bonus token, and 1 point on her report card. She is to start her next assignment at 0905. She is to be paid for this assignment in exactly the same way as in the first hour.

If she has earned the two tokens for working and the two bonus tokens (with the points on the report card) at 1000, she gets 1/2-hour break to do what she wants and free conversation with a staff member if she wants. If not, she should continue working after only a 5-minute break with no conversation. If she has earned the 1/2-hour break at 1000, she resumes work at 1030 and works till 1130 with the same contingencies as scheduled for 0800–0900 (explained above).

Her I.T. assignment is scheduled for 1300–1500. She gets one token per hour for this. If she does not go to I.T., she loses her tokens. If she is "pesky" during this time, put it on extinction, do not respond to her in any way. At 1500–1600, Carol has no work assignment, *but* she earns a point on her report card and a bonus token if she is not pesky. During P.M.'s she earns 1 point and 1 bonus token and 5 minutes of free conversation for each hour she refrains from being pesky. The last hour is 2100–2200. She can *also* earn up to 3 tokens for work during P.M.'s. This is to be negotiated between Carol and the P.M.'s what she is to earn the tokens for or whether she is to earn the tokens. Remember, she doesn't have to work in the P.M.'s and the work tokens she earns during P.M.'s do not count as points on the report card.

A summary of possible points she earns on her report card is as follows:

3 for acceptable work in the morning (1 per hour)
3 for refraining from pesky behavior in the morning (1 per hour)
3 for maintaining neat appearance (1 per hour)
7 for refraining from pesky behavior in the P.M.
___
16 total points.

You decided that the retarded women's problem with stimulus generalization could have been helped by all of the three means listed. Correct.

The essential ingredients in each of the programs are (1) agents of reinforcement who are trained to use the principles of shaping and contingency and (2) an environment which contains the relevant stimuli to be mastered by the patients. Let's try another example.

Mr. Blue, a chronic psychotic, progressed through a token economy and learned grooming, social, and occupational skills. Soon after he was discharged to a foster home he was returned to the hospital because of his bizarre habit of leaving the bathroom door open when using the toilet. His foster family felt he was "sick" again and brought him for re-admission.

The reason for Mr. Blue's bizarre habit was:

He was expressing his hostility to his foster family and expressing his wish to return to the hospital.....................................turn to page 239.

There were no doors on the toilet stalls in the hospital so he never learned the social propriety of keeping the bathroom door closed .... turn to page 241.

Old habits are hard to unlearn. You evidently have forgotten some of the message in Part I of this book. When you attribute Mr. Blue's failure to close the bathroom door to latent hostility and a wish to be returned to the hospital, you are engaging in inferential speculation. You may be right, but let's try to account more specifically and parsimoniously for his behavior. Let's not get involved guessing Mr. Blue's underlying motives until we've explored a more obvious and practical reason for his open door policy.

Return to page 237 and choose the right answer.

Very good. You decided that simple stimulus generalization could account for Mr. Blue's bizarre habit of leaving the bathroom door open when using the toilet. You probably have visited mental hospitals where the toilet stalls were without doors, ostensibly to facilitate observation of patients by the staff. This vignette about Mr. Blue shows why it is important to design the living environment in the hospital so it conforms to the standards outside the hospital . . . unless of course there is no interest in moving the patients back into the community. Open toilet stalls are designed perfectly for the values and goals of custodial institutions.

Let's move on to another type of token economy where juvenile delinquents were rehabilitated. Turn to page 243.

In a program of behavior therapy at the National Training School for Boys in Washington, D.C., reinforcement techniques were used to stimulate academic achievement (Cohen, 1967). In this penal institution conventional rewards for learning (grades, promotions, diploma) previously failed to motivate the inmates. The basic behavioral principle underlying the project is that academic behavior can be established and maintained by setting up an ecology in which positive consequences or rewards are made contingent upon gradually increasing educational performance.

The inmates, ranging in age from 14 to 18, were *employed* by the project staff as "Student Educational Researchers." The students were given points, convertible to money, as they successfully completed programmed instruction in such subjects as history, mathematics, foreign languages, grammar and literature, and in technical courses such as electricity, carpentry, and computer programming. To gain points, the student had to demonstrate 90% accuracy in a unit of instruction. A student could convert his points to the purchase of personal articles in a store; entry into a lounge containing a juke box, vending machines, and TV; rental of a private office where he could study; purchase of non-institutional food; and purchase of airline tickets for furloughs home.

As time went on, the students could spend their points on purchasing extra instructional programs, worth additional points, which they could work on during leisure hours. Initially 20 hours a week of programmed material was made available, but the students demanded more and the hours increased to 24, 32, then 40 and finally the school unit had to be kept open evenings as well.

A point-system economy on a ward for soldiers with character disorders has been running successfully for three years at the Walter Reed General Hospital. Learning situations are constructed so that the behavioral deficits of the soldiers can be remedied in a stepwise fashion. The milieu is structured as a military unit so that changes in behavior will generalize to the men's next duty assignment. Treatment goals are carefully specified in the areas of educational, recreational and social skills—two hours per day of courses are offered by staff and patients on such topics as public speaking, automobile repair, sex, and first aid, a unit work project is designed by the soldiers—for instance rebuilding an army post's stables and flying club—and points are awarded for working effectively in a group toward a common goal; the soldiers are given points for exercising leadership and for participating in the ward organization.

Participation is voluntary and if a soldier wishes he may spend his day doing nothing except eating, sleeping, and moving about as he pleases. However, if a soldier participates in activities he earns points which are convertible into privileges such as TV, billiards, snacks, and permission for leaves and passes. "Thus the unit utilizes an artificial extrinsic reinforcement system, a 'point economy' in which natural reinforcers in the system are paid for by points earned in daily activities within the therapeutic structure of the program. The men plan daily and weekly earning strategies; that is, they make behavioral decisions which will influence the reinforcement available to them in the future, a gratification model requiring increasing delay as they progress in treatment." (Colman & Baker, 1969.)

A savings bank was set up with interest provided so that students could learn "savings" behavior. Points could not be transferred from one student to another—so stealing, bribery, and extortion were prevented.

The physical environment was designed to elicit and maintain desired academic and social behaviors and reduce the likelihood of interfering behaviors. A cottage was remodeled to provide individual sleeping quarters with different degrees of comfort costing corresponding amounts of points. Classrooms and a library were built, as well as private offices with telephones. A private office cost students the equivalent of $40 per week for a person on a salary of $60 per week. The architecture favored studying. Institutional behavior such as pacing, boredom, and abject compliance with aversive authority was minimized.

Psychopaths and juvenile delinquents are said to be unable to delay gratification. Stated in the language of behavior analysis, these individuals:

Have certain behaviors which are not controlled by delayed reinforcement contingencies ....turn to page 249.

Are responsive to only *immediate* positive reinforcement or punishment......
....turn to page 247.

You say that delinquents and psychopaths are responsive only to immediate reward or punishment. Unfortunately this simple view of their psychopathology leaves out much of what we know to be true. For instance, punishment—even when applied immediately following the undesired act—has been notoriously unsuccessful in preventing recidivism. While punishment alone tells the subject what is not desired, it gives no information on what is positively desired. Thus, there is little chance for alternate, adaptive behavior to appear. Also, punishment frequently serves paradoxically as positive reinforcement since its properties of attentiveness and concern may outweigh its aversiveness.

It is more accurate to view delinquents and psychopaths as being able to defer gratification in some areas of behavior—such as in lengthy planning of criminal acts—but not in other areas, such as job and academic performances.

Return to page 245 and choose the correct answer.

Crucial to the success of token economies is the degree of administrative control exercised by the project staff in distributing rewards in a consistent and systematic way to the patients. If other sources of reward exist for the patients, particularly if the requirements of the competing source of reward are in contradiction to the goals of the project, the effectiveness of the token system will be impaired or completely lost. This situation can develop from within the token economy itself such as when a staff member intentionally or unintentionally sabotages the contingencies of reinforcement by dispensing tokens to patients when they do not deserve them, or forgetting to provide the tokens when they are deserved.

A token economy set up at a Job Corps center failed because the corpsmen were exposed to the system only part of the time. They were reinforced for constructive work accomplishments and for verbal participation in group meetings but when they returned to their dormitories, competing goals set up by the peer group canceled out the effects. Other programs have encountered difficulties when the cooperation of influential administrative echelons has not been engaged. For a program to work, all staff hierarchies, ranging from the superintendent through the nursing supervisors to those who provide food and janitorial services, must be involved in a common pursuit of the goals. A social systems approach to the administration of token economies is necessary with the project director sensitive to the influences bearing on the patients and staff from all directions.

We know that psychopaths and delinquents can work on criminal plans for long time periods before receiving a pay-off. Setting strategy for a bank robbery or hatching plans for a prison escape involve delays in gratification. Other behaviors however, such as educational and occupational performances do not long survive a delay in reinforcement. We might speculate that such adaptive behaviors have rarely been reinforced—even on an immediate basis —in delinquents and hence have never entered their behavioral repertoires.

In the National Training School project, contingencies are programmed to bring pro-social areas of conduct under the control of delayed reinforcement. The points (reinforcement) for academic behavior are initially given out immediately upon completion of a task, but at later stages in the program a student receives his points after a week or a semester. The students also learn to work for delayed reinforcement by having the incentive to save points for later purchase of expensive rewards, such as a phonograph or an airplane ticket for a home visit.

The achievements of the students in this project can be assessed in other ways besides their completion of academic courses and their successful adjustment to the point economy. Over an eight-month period the 28 students gained, on the average, a year grade level in reading, spelling, and arithmetic. On the average, they gained twelve points in IQ. These and other measures of progress are highly statistically significant. Although the program was designed to improve academic behavior, the social behavior of the students also changed. Disciplinary problems rarely occurred and the students began to model their speech and dress after the staff. Perhaps the best indication of the program's success is the fact that the new Federal Training School which has recently opened in West Virginia has incorporated many of the features of the point economy into its administrative operation.

SUMMARY OF CHAPTER 12

1. The token economy is a therapeutic milieu based on reinforcement principles. Patients earn tokens by showing improvement in their social, grooming, and work behavior. The tokens are then exchanged for items, consumables, activities and privileges that the patients desire.

2. The token economy brings the contingencies which operate in the "real world" into the wards of mental hospitals.

3. A technique used effectively is increasing some desirable behavior which initially occurs infrequently by making the opportunity to engage in some high frequency behavior contingent upon it.

4. Individualized programs of reinforcement as well as shaping procedures are used in token economies.

5. Token economies have been used to improve the behavior of various types of patients, including chronic psychotics, retardates, and delinquents.

Chapter 13: BEHAVIOR THERAPY WITH SCHIZOPHRENIC CHILDREN

The ability of behavioral techniques to modify abnormal behavior has been put to its severest test in behavior therapist's work with autistic and schizophrenic children. These children are incredibly isolated and unresponsive to conventional psychotherapeutic interventions and have very bizarre repertoires of behavior. They engage in prolonged periods of self-stimulatory activity, such as rocking, spinning, flapping of the arms, and fondling themselves. More dangerously, many of them are severely self-destructive. They have been observed to bite themselves, sometimes ripping out pieces of flesh down to the bone, blind themselves by gouging at their eyes, and engage in persistent head-banging to the point of causing subdural hematomas. Many of them have been kept in continuous restraint for literally years. The autistic child exhibits little or no social behavior and has a tremendous impoverishment of speech—some are mute, others echolalic.

About ten years ago psychologists began studying these children from the point of view of an experimental analysis of behavior. It was discovered that they could learn and that their behavior did change *if* their environment was programmed properly to provide them immediately with rewards contingent upon the desired changes. The rewards they responded to were food and candy, not attention, affection or praise from adults. Thus, these children not only have major deficits and excesses in their behavior, but they also are deficient in their response to social rewards. What reinforces behavior in normal children fails to affect the behavior of autistic children.

Ricky is an 11-year-old autistic child who, because of severe self-mutilative behavior, has spent his last seven years with both his arms and legs completely restrained. He has hit himself so hard and often that open sores exist on his cheeks and the back of his head which frequently bleed profusely. He has also broken his nose. In the past, whenever he has been removed from restraints he almost immediately attacks himself. This results in nursing staff rushing to him, holding him, reassuring him and putting him back into restraints. After being transferred to a behavior therapy unit, Ricky received care which resulted in the termination of his self-destructive behavior. Which procedure worked?

Ricky was released from his restraints and placed alone in a padded seclusion room where he was unable to see any of the staff. He spent one hour a day in the room until his attacks upon himself ceased..................turn to page 259.

Ricky was released from restraints and given a great deal of tender-loving-care. The nursing staff spent one hour a day with him, reassuring him that he was a good boy and that he didn't have to hit himself. These affection sessions continued until he no longer attacked himself when released from the restraints....
....turn to page 257.

There is no better way to insure that self-mutilative behavior will continue than to proceed in this manner. In fact, giving Ricky sympathy contingent upon his attacking himself was the means by which his attacks were maintained during the preceding seven years. He got the greatest attention from the nursing staff when he was released from restraints and began to flail himself. This intermittent schedule of reinforcement made his self-destruction behavior highly resistant to extinction.

Return to page 255 and choose the correct answer.

Operant conditioning methods have been used to instill greater self-help skills in autistic and other institutionalized children. Metz (1968) describes his work in teaching hospitalized children to wash their own hands before dinner.

We begin by stationing two adults at the dining room door. As each child comes in his way is blocked. A poker chip is placed in his hand and then his hand, with chip in it, is guided to the token box held by the second adult. He is shown how to deposit the chip into the box, and then immediately ushered into the dining room. Gradually, the distance between the chip giver and the chip taker is increased until the children are going out of their way to obtain the chips. At this point the chip giver is in the bathroom, and he begins gradually imposing work requirements on the children for which they are paid a chip. First, they are rewarded simply for placing a hand under the running water. Gradually the requirements are increased until a whole sequence of responses are made including washing with soap, drying, depositing the paper towel in the waste basket, taking a chip, and depositing it in the token box (now unmanned) near the dining room door. Finally, the chips and token box are eliminated so that the children can carry out the routine independently with a minimum of supervision. The special personnel needed to establish this routine can now be employed for establishing independence in other routines such as dressing, and grooming. The overall effect of such training creates a sense of order and a feeling of self-control in these extremely disorganized children, provide them with socially and personally useful skills, create a more emotionally satisfactory atmosphere during each of these activities, and free nursing personnel for more creative work with the children.*

* Reprinted with permission of the author and Scientific Publications, Department of Mental Hygiene, State of California, from Operant Conditioning in Behavior Therapy: Some Illustrations and Reflections in *California Mental Health Research Symposium No. 2*, 1968. Copyright © 1968 by Scientific Publications.

You are apparently well aware that environmental stimuli are crucial in maintaining self-mutilation. The attention and sympathy that self-destructive behavior generates in nursing staff clearly reinforces the very behavior the staff wish to turn off. Placing Ricky in isolation, led to an initial increase in the intensity of his hitting himself, but gradually the rate of hitting decreased and then stopped entirely. You will recognize this as an extinction procedure; that is, reinforcement which maintains the problem is withdrawn. There is a great deal of variation among children in how long extinction takes to eliminate this behavior. Because some children can conceivably kill themselves if allowed to gradually extinguish, another technique has been added. In addition to the interpersonal isolation, a painful but harmless electric shock was given to the child when he began to hit himself. This quickly led to cessation of the hitting and the duration of cessation tends to be lasting after just a few trials. If the therapist pairs a loud "No" with the shock, the reprimand itself becomes an effective stimulus in stopping subsequent self-attacks.

Lovaas (1967) who has done the most extensive work with autistic children, points out that

> every conceivable form of treatment had been tried on these children, to no avail. Further, our data indicate that traditional treatment involving the communication of support and affection for the child when he is self-destructive, makes him worse. It is apparent, then, that definitions of an affectionate or punitive relationship between the child and those who care for him cannot be made in terms of how one behaves toward the child, but rather in terms of the effect of one's interventions upon the child. To show affection to a child who is self-destructive is to aggress on him. To deliver pain to diminish a child's self-destruction is to demonstrate affection to him.

The occasional use of benign electric shock has resulted in other therapeutic gains as well. We will discuss this on page 261.

One way of making approval, attention and affection from adults rewarding to autistic children is to pair biological rewards (food, candy) with some indication that the children are responding to social events. In retraining their patients toward more socialized responsiveness, Lovaas (1967) gave the children food only when they systematically responded to social events. In other words, the child's attentiveness to adults was reinforced with food. However, this method proved tedious and impractical.

Lovaas and his co-workers then attempted to establish adult attention as rewarding by associating this with the termination of pain. Their reasoning went this way:

> We assumed that a great deal of meaning and reward value in interpersonal relationships come about because people mediate the termination of anxiety for each other. A child's love for his parent may be largely a function of his parent's help when he is frightened. That is, by removing the fright, the parent comes to signal rescue; hence the parent himself may take on positive rewarding qualities. Throughout life, the parent intervenes in this manner with his children. When the child demonstrates some biological stress, during his first year, the parent often picks him up, cuddles him, and is instrumental in removing biological discomforts. Later on in life the child will turn to his parents for help when he is experiencing interpersonal stress, failures in school, nightmares, and so on.

Initially painful but harmless electric shock and later slaps were given to the autistic children when they exhibited self-stimulatory or self-destructive behavior and was immediately terminated as soon as the children made some social response. Any approximation to a social response such as merely looking at one of the therapists was reinforced by the termination of the shock. In this way, pain onset served to suppress unwanted behavior and pain offset functioned to strengthen desired social behavior.

Extract from J. Richard Metz's "Operant Conditioning in Behavior Therapy: Some Illustrations and Reflections," in *California Mental Health Research Symposium No. 2*, 1968:

A misconception of operant conditioning goes like this: Operant conditioning is an undesirable method of changing behavior because it manipulates from without rather than encouraging interest in a task for its own sake. External control is exercised by the environment such that the individual loses his freedom and sense of self-determination. Such visions of a darkly Machiavellian method disturb those of us who value the democratic ideals of self-determination and freedom from coercion. In my experience, at least with severely disturbed children, we usually begin with an individual who is already relatively devoid of self control and who is largely at the mercy of his environment. He is a truly isolated individual. We have little influence over him, but by the same token he has little influence over us. Although we initiate the training procedure, I think it is helpful to look at the behavior therapy process as an interaction between patient and therapist which leads step by step to an ever increasing ability of *each to influence the other*. I sometimes wisecrack to my assistants as we turn summersaults to reinforce a patient that I am not sure just who is conditioning whom. As the child learns social skills, how to think more logically, how to use language, how to discuss and persuade, he comes increasingly under the control of his social environment, to be sure, but he exerts similar control over his environment. He becomes, as we say, more truly independent.*

* Reprinted with permission of the author and Scientific Publications, Department of Mental Hygiene, State of California, from Operant Conditioning in Behavior Therapy: Some Illustrations and Reflections in *California Mental Health Research Symposium No. 2*, 1968. Copyright © 1968 by Scientific Publications.

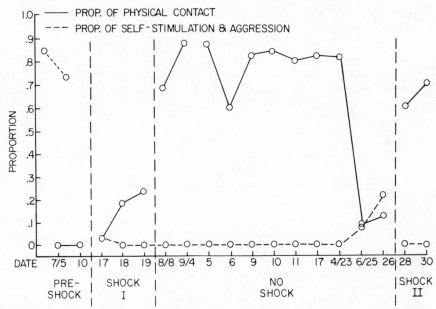

Fig. 7. The use of shock to generate social behavior in a self-aggressive autistic child. (From Lovaas, O. I., Schaefer, B., & Simmons, J. Q. Experimental Studies in Childhood Schizophrenia: Building Social Behavior in Autistic Children by Use of Electric Shock. *J. Exptl. Research in Personality*, 1965, Vol. 1, p. 105. Copyright Academic Press, New York, 1965.)

The final step in this procedure was to bring together a host of social stimuli from the therapists and associate them with termination of pain, thereby helping the therapists to become positive reinforcers in the future. As soon as the child showed some social response and the pain was removed, the therapist would take the child into his arms, kissing and hugging him. The use of slaps and spankings supplanted the more experimental efforts with electric shock because they more closely approximated real-life experiences and hence would be more likely to produce generalized effects outside the hospital. Figure 7 shows data from one patient treated by Lovaas (1967) with the effect of shock on pathological behaviors and social behaviors.

The strengthening of social behavior by making removal of pain contingent upon its appearance is an example of:

> Negative reinforcement
> Punishment
> Positive reinforcement

Turn to page 265 for the correct answer.

If you chose negative reinforcement you are correct. The procedure is one in which a particular behavior is increased by the contingent removal of an aversive stimulus. Punishment is defined as the *weakening* of some behavior as a result of its being met by aversive consequences. In both negative reinforcement and punishment, an aversive stimulus operates as the motivating force. For negative reinforcement to occur, the individual must have an opportunity to behave in a way which will permit avoidance or escape from the aversive stimulus. In punishment, there is no escape route and the behavior which leads to the "pain" is diminished. Positive reinforcement refers to the process by which some action is increased in frequency because it generates positive consequences or rewards. If you are a little rusty on the basic behavioral definitions, go back over the material in Chapter 3 for a review.

One of the exciting new extensions of behavior therapy with children that has major implications for community mental health and preventive psychiatry is the teaching of behavioral principles to parents. Seminars and workshops have been sponsored by behavior therapists at university centers and by national associations of parents with emotionally-disturbed children. Using didactic presentations, films, and practical demonstrations, the parents are taught the basic principles of reinforcement, extinction, discrimination training, and shaping. They are given homework assignments which require them to pinpoint the problem behaviors and the desired goals with their children and then to keep records of progress made when employing behavioral interventions.

There are two excellent programmed manuals which illustrate behavioral principles with case examples (Patterson & Gullion, 1968; Smith & Smith, 1966). Reports have been made of the success of parent workshops (Walder, 1966; Lovaas, 1967) and plans are being made to extend these educational opportunities to parents of newborns in an effort to prevent behavioral disorders from starting. The parents are the logical people to employ behavioral techniques since they provide the crucial reinforcement for their children and have the responsibility to choose reasonable goals.

Autistic and schizophrenic children have notorious deficits in their use of language. Many are mute, and still others are only able to echo back what someone has said. All of them show inadequate use of abstract speech.

Behavior therapists, pioneered by the work of Lovaas, have made substantial progress in helping these children develop communicative verbal skills. The first step in the language "program" is teaching a child to imitate words. Imitation is a major process by which normal children acquire speech and other complex behavior. Lovaas (1967) describes the steps of successive discriminations involved in verbal imitation training:

Step 1: Reinforce any vocalization made by the child to increase total vocal output.

Step 2: Reinforce the child for vocal behavior only when it is in response to the therapist's speech.

Step 3: Reinforce finer discrimination by rewarding the child only when he precisely matches the therapist's sounds.

Step 4: Repeat Step 3 with another sound, demanding increasingly fine discriminations and reproductions from the child before rewarding him.

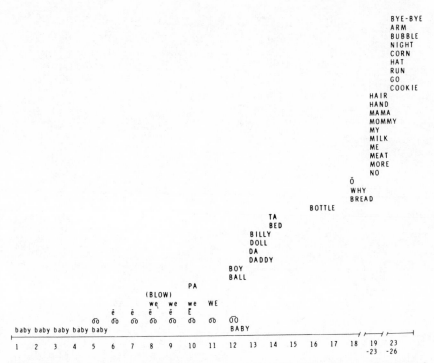

Fig. 8. The acquisition of a vocabulary by an autistic child. (From Lovaas, O. I., *et al.* Acquisition of Imitative Speech in Schizophrenic Children. *Science*, Vol. 151, p. 706, Feb. 11, 1966. Copyright 1966 by the American Association for the Advancement of Science.)

Following these steps and starting with clearly different sounds (e.g., the consonant "m" and the vowel "o"), the child is gradually taught to imitate a wider and wider range of sounds, words, and sentences. Verbal training starts with imitation where the child learns to discriminate by being differentially reinforced for his gradual improvement. Therapists have found that children positively accelerate in their acquisition of new words so that after twenty to thirty days the child can imitate almost any sound that is presented to him. The acquisition curve for one child treated by Lovaas is shown in Fig. 8.*

Because imitation of sounds and words received reinforcement, the pairing process led to a situation where imitative behavior itself developed rewarding qualities. As Lovaas (1967) stated:

> After certain stages of learning had been acquired, the children would improve

* Reprinted with permission of the American Association for the Advancement of Science, Washington, D.C.

in their enunciation of words without extrinsic reinforcement. This finding contrasts markedly with the popular stereotype of the conditioning product, namely that of a robot or automaton who is unable to function independently. Our experiments show clearly that the children can, at certain stages of learning, acquire new behaviors on their own by merely listening and looking.

After mastering imitation of speech, the autistic child still must learn to attach meaning to words —a case of discriminative learning. This is accomplished by teaching the child the appropriate context for the use of language. The first step is to help the child to label or describe his environment, including his own behavior and that of others. Initially the child is taught to label simple objects—to call meat "meat," and dog "dog." Later more elaborate discriminations are developed, involving the establishment of time concepts, prepositions, and pronouns.

The second step is to teach the children to behave in accord with verbal cues in the environment. Following instructions and asking for objects or food are mastered during this stage of the language program. An example of this would be giving a child a toy when he says, "Please give me the toy." The third step is teaching conversation to the children. Here they learn to speak and listen intelligibly; for example, a child might be taught to name the pieces of furniture in the room when asked, "What kinds of furniture are there in the room?" They also learn spontaneity by reinforcing them when they relate their feelings and their immediate reactions to events.

Lovaas (1967) describes the process:

> These discriminations are built in very gradual steps and involve extensive use of prompts and fading techniques. That is, since the children could not emit the correct verbal behavior or did not know how to behave non-verbally, we prompted the correct response by telling the child what it was, moving him physically through the correct behavior, or otherwise actively helping him behave correctly. In successive steps these prompts would be faded, the adult participating less and less in the child's behavior, until the child could emit the correct behavior in the mere presence of the appropriate stimulus. Employing this paradigm, we have proceeded in a step-by-step fashion to teach the children appropriate use of response to concepts involving size, color, shape, prepositions, pronouns, and time.

SUMMARY OF CHAPTER 13

1. Autistic or schizophrenic children pose major challenges to behavior modification because they have extreme deficits and excesses in their behavioral repertoires.

2. Programming the environment of these children so that rewards and punishments are made systematically contingent upon desired and undesired behavior respectively leads to therapeutic change.

3. Painful but harmless electric shock when applied contingent on the exhibition of severely self-mutilative behavior, quickly and reliably stops this life-threatening behavior. Pairing shock with positive reinforcement of socially appropriate behavior is most effective in producing lasting therapeutic gains.

4. Imitation and reinforcement have been used successfully to build communicative language in mute and echolalic children.

Chapter 14: OPERANT TECHNIQUES IN THE CLASSROOM

Praise, recognition and attention offered by teachers serve to effectively reinforce students' behavior on which it focuses. Behavior can be reinforced in desirable or undesirable directions depending upon when and how the teacher's attention is dispensed. Most teachers begin their careers with little experience and competence in keeping a class of children in reasonable control. Some teachers learn methods of control intuitively and quickly; others never learn and thus do little effective teaching. The development of reinforcement methods for modifying maladaptive classroom behaviors offers the promise of making this long-neglected domain of educational technique teachable to all. A wide variety of maladaptive student behaviors have been modified including crying, dependency on the teacher, absence of play, poor peer relationships, tantrums, extreme aggression, inarticulate use of language, hyperactivity, and wild, disruptive social play (O'Leary *et al.*, 1969; Harris *et al.*, 1964; Thomas *et al.*, 1968; Homme, 1969; Madsen, 1970).

One important and generally used strategy to demonstrate the social reinforcement power of the teacher involves five stages. The first stage consists of a period of observation of the student(s) in order to get a baseline record of behavior. The observations are usually focused on the problem behaviors and alternate, more appropriate behaviors. Also measured are the responses the teacher makes to the students.

During the second stage, the teacher is taught to change her pattern of responsiveness to the students. If, for example, she had been attending to undesirable behavior by scolding, she now completely ignores it. She is neither punitive nor offended, but simply shuts her eyes and ears to it. If she previously had been inattentive to desirable, but infrequent, behavior she now sets out to systematically detect and reinforce every instance of it. The second stage continues until the teacher succeeds in producing the desired change in the students. Children are extremely sensitive to attention from the teacher and the method almost always succeeds. On occasions when attention contingent upon desired behavior does not produce a salutary effect, other methods such as token reinforcement are used. The tokens (*see* previous chapter) serve as conditioned reinforcers and can be exchanged by the students for candy, pennies, or toys.

The third stage is a return to the original conditions of the baseline period. The teacher is instructed to resume responding to her students in her customary way. This "reversal" stage proves that the contingencies of reinforce-

ment were responsible for the change in behavior. When the teacher reverses her focus of attention, the children will reverse their behavior and regress toward the baseline. Although the reversal stage is used, in part, for purposes of research "proof," it also gives the teacher confidence in her ability to construct an optimal environment for her students through the selective use of her attentiveness and praise. As scientific evidence for the use of contingency management in classrooms accumulates, this reversal stage may be eliminated.

During the fourth stage, the teacher reinstates her focusing on "good" behavior—the experimental procedure which proved effective during the second stage. Typically, the children recover the desired behavior quickly. The fifth stage involves techniques which are aimed at making the desirable behavior more durable and able to be generalized. The teacher switches from continuous to intermittent reinforcement and substitutes more natural forms of reinforcement for her attention. Natural reinforcement may derive from other students in the class offering praise or recognition for more desirable behavior or from the intrinsic satisfaction that the former problem child now obtains from engaging in academic or social play activities.

The substance of these behavior modification studies are the ordinary but potent forms of attention given by teachers—glances, smiles, nods, watching, as well as direct verbal responses to behavior. What the teacher supplies to the students is not altered; solely the "when" is changed.

One example will suffice to illustrate the method. A four-year-old girl who was extremely withdrawn and adult-oriented was reinforced with praise by her nursery school teacher for child-oriented responses. Shaping the girl's involvement with peers required the teacher to initially reinforce the girl's simply looking at other children. To provide more opportunities for positive reinforcement, the teacher primed her for interactions by getting other children into the girl's play area. Within a relatively brief period, the child's interactions with peers more than tripled. During the third or reversal stage, the child's involvement with other pupils dropped precipitously despite the presence of other children in her immediate play area. Contact with peers was quickly reinstated during stage four when the teacher resumed praising her for socializing with other children. The girl's playing and cooperating with other children was solidified by switching to intermittent reinforcement and by the children and the social games taking over the reinforcing function from the teacher.

Robbie was a particularly disruptive pupil who studied very little. A baseline record revealed that Robbie studied during only 25 percent of the observational intervals (studying was defined as having pencil on paper for five seconds or more of a ten-second interval). The behaviors which filled the other 75 percent of the intervals were snapping rubber bands, playing with toys from his pocket, talking and laughing with classmates, slowly drinking his milk and then playing with the empty carton afterwards. During the baseline period, the teacher was observed often encouraging Robbie to work or chiding him for dawdling and talking. Over half the attention Robbie received from his teacher was for non-study behavior.

Robbie's dawdling and disruptive behavior:

Was a result of a problem he had at home and of insufficient maturity to function in a classroom setting.................................turn to page 283.

Was a consequence of the inadvertent contingencies of reinforcement provided by his teacher...turn to page 285.

Don't allow yourself to make interpretations based on Robbie's home-life. Robbie might very well have problems with his parents or siblings, but we are focusing on problem behaviors that are manifest in the classroom. Let's first see if there are good reasons in the school setting for Robbie's misbehavior before we jump to conclusions about causes in his home. You are given a clue with the information about how Robbie's teacher focuses attention on non-study behavior.

As for the explanatory value of "insufficient maturity (or ego strength) to function in a classroom," what more is meant by this than the simple restatement of Robbie's problem? All too often, the terms "immaturity" or "poor ego strength" serve as wastebaskets into which is stuffed the frustrated ineffectiveness of teachers and therapists.

Return to page 281 and re-read the material carefully before selecting the correct answer.

You said that Robbie's difficulties in class stemmed from improper contingencies of reinforcement provided by his teacher. Absolutely correct! You have a good grasp on the functional analysis of behavior. With over 50% of teacher's attention directed towards Robbie's non-study behavior, it is not at all surprising that he dawdles and disrupts. Daydreaming and intrusive acts by students are the bane of teachers and seem almost reflexively to draw reprimands and exhortations. With some teachers, practically their entire verbal repertoire consists of admonitions, commands, and reprimands. If only they knew how their efforts to reduce disruptive behavior paradoxically serve to increase it!

Turn to the next page to find out how Robbie's problem was remedied.

To start Robbie on the path to better study habits his teacher came to him whenever he had worked for one minute and made an approving comment such as, "Very good work, Robbie. I see you are studying." At the same time she stopped attending to dawdling and disruptive behaviors. During the next fifteen sessions, he was observed studying 71 percent of the time. When the experimental contingencies were dropped during a brief reversal phase, his study rate dipped to 50 percent of the time. Reinstating reinforcement for studying resulted in a rise to 80 percent. Follow-up checks made 14 weeks after the teacher stopped receiving cues from the observer showed that Robbie had maintained his improvement. His teacher also reported that he was completing his assignments and missing fewer words on spelling tests.

You should not take away the impression that all classroom problems can be treated like Robbie's. Problems differ and their solutions require individualized approaches. The general principles are the same—specify the problem in concrete, behavioral ways and attach reinforcing consequences to the desired goals. The reinforcers may differ from student to student. For many, praise and recognition from the teacher may be sufficient. For others, tokens will work. Still others may improve only when the contingencies for the entire class are changed, particularly if the problem is being maintained by the recognition it provokes from fellow students.

A skeptic might object to our jumping to the conclusion that the systematic and selective use of attention by the teacher is the best way to obtain classroom control. Behavior problems in the school are so perennial and time-consuming that it hardly seems likely that some simple way to resolve them could be found. Let's encourage skepticism by reporting an experiment which is designed to tease out the factors involved in classroom control (Madsen et al., 1968).

Public school teachers were instructed to introduce two different conditions in consecutive order, for the purpose of instilling classroom discipline. First, they were to provide a set of brief but specific rules for good classroom behavior and to have the children recite them at least five times a day. The rules were posted conspicuously in the room and consisted of such things as, "Sit quietly while working." At a later time, the teachers were instructed in how to use praise selectively for appropriate classroom behavior.

Two problem children were observed carefully during the experimental periods as well as during other periods when the teacher either ignored misbehavior or returned to the baseline conditions where intuitive methods of control were used. The intuitive methods were scolding or reminding the child of his disruptiveness. Observations of appropriate and inappropriate behavior were made with a reliable rating code for twenty minutes, three times a week for 25 weeks.

One child, Cliff, was described by his teacher as sitting "throughout entire work periods fiddling with objects in his desk, talking, doing nothing, or misbehaving by bothering others and walking around the room. Lately he has started hitting others for no apparent reason—I was unable to motivate him into working on any task during the regular school periods." The other problem child, Frank, frequently misbehaved in class by fighting, being out of his seat, and talking to other children.

What do you suppose happened when Cliff and Frank were exposed to the various experimental procedures? Did the relating of explicit rules and expectations produce a beneficial effect on their classroom behavior? How about the ignoring of misbehavior—did this lead to improvement? How important was the differential use of praise and approval contingent upon "good," attentive study behavior?

Decide what effects each of these methods had and then turn to page 291 and find out what really happened.

A possible objection to the use of behavior modification methods in the classroom might be that, despite their effectiveness, they produce feelings of powerlessness and dehumanization in the students. The stereotype of conditioning methods making robots out of people is harbored by many mental health professionals and educators who have heard about, but not seen the results of behavior modification.

Concerned with the above emotional reactions to behavior modification programs, investigators have begun to assess the possibility of adverse "side-effects" of these programs. One study, utilizing intelligence and projective tests, found no adverse effects in children whose specific deviant behavior was reduced by reinforcement techniques (Ward & Baker, 1968). The same authors found no deterioration in the behavior of the other pupils in the class when the teacher focused on treating four problem children.

Another group of investigators (Graubard et al., 1969) interviewed boys who had participated in a behavior modification program in a residential center for disturbed delinquents. The program included a group contingency; that is, if each student fulfilled his work assignment, everyone benefited with a larger reward. The interviews explored informally what effect the experience had on their feelings about school, teachers, and themselves. The students' comments were enthusiastic and positive. Comments about the teacher included, "She didn't hold us down," "She let us work at our own level," and, "She tells you when you're right." The students all felt that they had learned with statements such as, "Everytime I passed a test, I'd get smarter and smarter," and "I earned that stuff . . . I had to hustle like a bitch."

Although more work in this area needs to be done, the early leads indicate that behavior modification produces favorable side-effects.

The graph shewn on page 293 depicts what actually happened to the frequency of inappropriate behavior exhibited by Cliff and Frank under the different conditions imposed by their teacher. During the baseline period, misbehavior occurred in an average of 47 percent of intervals in which observations were made. Rules had little effect on the frequency of misbehavior. During the time that the teacher ignored their cutting-up, its frequency increased.

A substantial, beneficial effect occurred only when selective praise for studying and pro-social behavior was added to the already posted rules. By the end of the experiment, misbehavior occurred in less than 15 percent of the observational intervals. Note that when the teacher reverted to the baseline conditions after using differential praise for almost seven weeks, the children's behavior markedly worsened.

After being trained in the selective use of positive reinforcement, the teacher remarked, "I was amazed at the difference the procedure made in the atmosphere of the classroom and even in my own personal feelings. I realized that in praising the well-behaved children and ignoring the bad, I was finding myself looking for the good in the children. It was rewarding to see the good rather than always criticizing. . . . I became convinced that a positive approach to discipline was the answer."

While systematic ratings were made only of the behavior of the two problem children, dramatic changes were seen in the other children as well. The authors conclude by stating: "Unless teachers are effective in getting children 'ready to learn,' their technical teaching skills are likely to be wasted. Knowledge of differential social reinforcement procedures as well as other behavioral principles, can greatly enhance teachers' enjoyment of the profession and their contributions to effective development of the students."

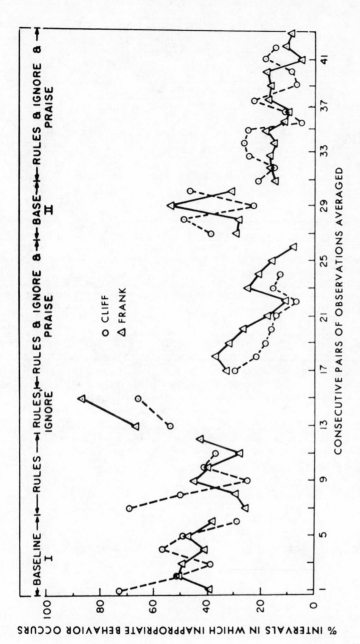

Fig. 9. The importance of positive reinforcement (praise) in the management of disruptive classroom behavior. (From Madsen, C. H., *et al.*, Rules, Praise, and Ignoring: Elements of Elementary Classroom Control. *Journal of Applied Behavior Analysis*, 1968, Vol. 1, 139–150. Copyright 1968 by the Society for the Experimental Analysis of Behavior, and reproduced with permission.)

Behavioral approaches are uniquely suited for application in ghetto schools. The specificity and concreteness of the approaches enable the teacher and student to bypass contrasts in social class and verbal styles. Discovering what is reinforcing for a ghetto child—such as the use of token reinforcers which can be exchanged for things valued by the child—can help to make education relevant and attractive.

One recent study utilized a behavioral principle to enhance the learning of pre-schoolers in a Head Start classroom (Jacobson *et al.*, 1969). The class, located in a community center gymnasium, was staffed by mothers of the students. The classroom was divided into activity areas—block area, manipulative toy area, creative materials area, climbing area, pre-reading area. One of the problems encountered in the class was the excessive switching from area to area. To reduce the disruptive behavior, a task requirement was introduced as a prerequisite for switching. Movement from one area to another required that the child first stop at a centrally placed table and complete simple color or word matching problems, an effort that was, under usual circumstances, given little preference by the children. Completion of the task resulted in the child receiving a ticket to enter an activity area of his choice. Each time a child wished to change areas, he first had to stop at the central station, complete a task, and receive a ticket.

From your knowledge of reinforcement principles, what effect would you estimate that the switching requirement had on frequency of moving from area to area?

Turn to page 297 to find the answer.

If you estimated that making switching from area to area contingent upon the completion of matching tasks led to a decrease in switching, you are correct. The children reduced the frequency of their moving from area to area from 3–5 per hour to 1–2 per hour. Several benefits accrued. The children increased their attention span on individual activities and involved themselves more intensively. They also learned colors and words which were required for switching. Finally, the mothers on the teaching staff were able to devote more time to individual instruction of children who were less distracted.

Do you remember the Premack Principle? If you do, you might interpret the results from the Head Start classroom just described as consonant with the Premack Principle. Behavior frequently engaged in (switching areas) was reduced by making it contingent upon behavior rarely emitted (completion of matching tasks).

SUMMARY OF CHAPTER 14

1. Praise, recognition and other forms of attention offered by teachers serve to effectively reinforce students' behavior on which it focuses.

2. Material reinforcers—such as candy, toys, extra time for play—can also assist the teacher in developing more adaptive social and academic behavior in the students. Token systems (*see* Chapter 12) have been used with great success.

3. Behavior modification techniques can aid the mental health consultant in efforts to facilitate primary and secondary prevention of behavioral disorders in his work with the educational system.

SUMMARY

You have completed a trip through the behavior therapy countryside. While your journey has been brief, I hope it has provided you with a comprehensive glimpse of the behavioral approach to clinical problems in mental health. If your appetite for more training, reading and direct experience with behavior therapy has been whetted, this book can be counted a success. The Annotated Bibliography at the end of the book will be a helpful starting point.

Training in behavior modification is offered at several universities on a graduate level. Western Michigan University, Southern Illinois University, State University of New York at Stony Brook, University of Kansas, and University of Illinois are the most notable among these. More informal workshops, courses, and seminars as well as consultation and supervision are offered frequently by schools, hospitals, and private agencies. One good source of information on training opportunities is the Association for the Advancement of Behavior Therapy (415 East 52nd Street, New York, New York 10022).

The ethical implications of behavior modification have not been emphasized in this book. The issues are complex and thorny but do deserve some comment. Because behavioral techniques are so effective in reaching treatment goals, the values which go into the formulating of the goals become crucially important. There are few absolute "goods" in the universe of mental health. We generally accept the view that behavior which is "adaptive" to the individual in his adjustment to his social milieu are desirable goals in treatment. However, conflict can easily appear in the definition of adjustment. For example, while it may be non-controversial for an enuretic child to be rid of his maladaptive symptom, there is considerable disagreement over the adaptiveness of such behaviors as protest demonstrations and violence against property by economically and politically deprived segments of the population (ghetto blacks, college students, American Indians). Some therapists even hew to the belief that the bizarre and irrational behavior of schizophrenics should not be interfered with but rather allowed to run its course naturally. Without belaboring the issue, behavior therapists have tended to choose relatively non-controversial goals for treatment using values that the vast majority of clinicians and citizens would agree with. Behavior therapists tend also to put their values out into the open so that scrutiny by peers and patients can lead to collaboration, constructive criticism, and a dialogue. This can be seen in the cases given in this book.

As behavior therapies increase in effectiveness, the responsibilities of those practicing these techniques will also increase in importance. No one should be so naive as to have unblinking faith in the humanitarian and altruistic behavior of therapists—professional societies and legal mechanisms will have to insure the propriety of their behavior. Behavior therapists, however, are more likely to place their own values on the table for all to see since they must explicate problems and goals with their patients. It may be worthwhile to encourage all therapists to indicate their values to their patients before beginning a course of treatment.

While the potency of behavior therapy in changing human behavior should beneficially raise concerns over the ethics and values of our clinical practice, another area of ethical concern has been given scant attention. Can we consider our continued use of traditional methods which have questionable effectiveness and low efficiency unethical? With new and effective treatment approaches now available, we can no longer justify using more time-consuming and costly therapies. Are we indeed committed to minimizing the suffering of our patients? Behavior therapy will be tested against more conventional techniques during the coming years in cost-effectiveness analyses. Then we will have some answers.

If the impression has been given in this book that behavior therapy always works and that there is a technique to solve every problem, the author apologizes. Examples were chosen which highlighted some of the more successful innovations in behavior modification, but behavior therapists have encountered their share of problems, impasses, and failures. What behavior therapists emphasize is their commitment to experiment with a wide variety of methods, and their empirical attitude which enables them to use the positive and negative results of their work to further refine the discipline. Behavioral technology has not developed to the point of a cook-book application to any and all problems encountered by clinicians. We look ahead to continued research and development of methods which work under specified conditions and with particular populations.

APPENDIX

BEHAVIORAL APPROACHES TO FAMILY AND COUPLE THERAPY

Robert Liberman, M.D.

Behavioral approaches to family therapy specify the problems in concrete and observable terms, empirically applying principles of learning in working toward therapeutic goals. The key to successful family therapy can be found in the changes made in the interpersonal consequences of the family members' behavior.

The current splurge of couple and family therapies is not simply an accident or passing fad. These increasingly used modes of treatment for psychiatric problems are anchored in a sound foundation and are not likely to blow away. The foundation of these newer therapies lies in the opportunity they offer to induce significant behavioral change in the participants by a major restructuring of their interpersonal environments.

Couple and family therapy can be particularly potent means of behavior modification because the interpersonal milieu that undergoes change is that of the day-to-day, face-to-face encounter an individual experiences with the most important people in his life—his spouse or members of his immediate family. When these therapies are successful it is because the therapist is able to guide the members of the couple or family into changing their modes of dealing with each other. In behavioral or learning terms, we can translate "ways of dealing with each other" into consequences of behavior or *contingencies of reinforcement*. Instead of rewarding maladaptive behavior with attention and concern, the family members learn to give each other recognition and approval for desired behavior.

Since the family is a system of interlocking, reciprocal behaviors (including affective behavior), family therapy proceeds best when each of the members learns how to change his or her responsiveness to the others. Family therapy should be a learning experience for all the members involved. For simplifica-

Reprinted from *American Journal of Orthopsychiatry*, January 1970, **40**, 1, 106–118. Copyright 1970, by the American Orthopsychiatric Association, Inc. Reproduced by permission. (Submitted to the *Journal* in January 1969.)

Dr. Liberman was a career officer in the NIMH Mental Health Career Development Program. Preparation of this paper was begun while he was a fellow in the research training program in social psychiatry at Harvard Medical School and Massachusetts Mental Health Center. He is now a Research Psychiatrist, Center for the Study of Behavioral Disorders, Camarillo State Hospital, Camarillo, California.

tion, however, this paper will analyze family pathology and therapy from the point of view of the family responding to a single member.

Typically, families that come for treatment have coped with the maladaptive or deviant behavior of one member by responding to it over the years with anger, nagging, babying, conciliation, irritation, or sympathy. These responses, however punishing they might seem on the surface, have the effect of reinforcing the deviance, that is, increasing the frequency or intensity of the deviant behavior in the future. Reinforcement occurs because the attention offered is viewed and felt by the deviant member as positive concern and interest. In many families with a deviant member, there is little social interaction and the individuals tend to lead lives relatively isolated from each other. Because of this overall lack of interaction, when interaction does occur in response to a member's "abnormal" behavior, such behavior is powerfully reinforced [14].

Verbal and non-verbal means of giving attention and recognition can be termed *social reinforcement* (as contrasted with food or sex, which are termed *primary reinforcement*). Social reinforcement represents the most important source of motivation for human behavior [6,19]. Often massive amounts of such "concern" or social reinforcement are communicated to the deviant member, focused and contingent upon the member's maladaptive behavior. The deviant member gets the message: "So long as you continue to produce this undesirable behavior (symptoms), we will be interested and concerned in you." Learning the lesson of such messages leads to the development and maintenance of symptomatic or deviant behavior and to characterological patterns of activity and identity. Sometimes, the message of concern and interest is within the awareness of the "sick" member. Individuals with a conscious awareness of these contingencies are frequently termed "manipulative" by mental health professionals since they are adept at generating social reinforcement for their maladaptive behavior. But learning can occur without an individual's awareness or insight, in which case we view the maladaptive behavior as being unconsciously motivated.

Massive amounts of contingent social reinforcement are not necessary to maintain deviant behavior. Especially after the behavior has developed, occasional or *intermittent reinforcement* will promote very durable continuation of the behavior. Laboratory studies have shown that intermittent reinforcement produces behavior that is most resistant to extinction [6].

Many family therapists [7,8,21] have demonstrated that the interest and concern family members show in the deviance of one member can be in the service of their own psychological economy. Maintaining a "sick" person in the family can be gratifying (reinforcing) to others, albeit at some cost in comfort and equanimity. Patterson [15] describes how this reciprocal reinforcement can maintain deviant behavior by using the example of a child who demands an ice cream cone while shopping with his mother in a supermarket.

The reinforcer for this "demand behavior" is compliance by the mother, but if she ignores the demand, the effect is to increase the rate or loudness of the demand. Loud demands or shrieks by a child in a supermarket are aversive to the mother; that is, her noncompliance is punished. When the mother finally buys the ice cream cone, the aversive tantrum ends. The reinforcer for the child's tantrum is the ice cream cone. The reinforcing contingency for the mother was the termination of the "scene" in the supermarket. In this reciprocal fashion, the tantrum behavior is maintained. I shall return to this important aspect of family psychopathology—the mutually reinforcing or symbiotic nature of deviance—in the case studies below. Indeed, the balance between the aversive and gratifying consequences of maladaptive behavior in a member on the other family members is the crucial determinant of motivation for and response to treatment.

Changing the contingencies by which the patient gets acknowledgment and concern from other members of his family is the basic principle of learning that underlies the potency of family or couple therapy. Social reinforcement is made contingent on desired, adaptive behavior instead of maladaptive and symptomatic behavior. It is the task of the therapist in collaboration with the family or couple to (1) specify the maladaptive behavior, (2) choose reasonable goals which are alternative, adaptive behaviors, (3) direct and guide the family to change the contingencies of their social reinforcement patterns from maladaptive to adaptive target behaviors.

Another principle of learning involved in the process of successful family therapy is modeling, also called imitation or identification. The model, sometimes the therapist but also other members of the family, exhibits desired, adaptive behavior which then is imitated by the patient. Imitation or identification occurs when the model is an esteemed person (therapist, admired family member) and when the model receives positive reinforcement (approval) for his behavior from others [3]. The amount of observational learning will be governed by the degree to which a family member pays attention to the modeling cues, has the capacity to process and rehearse the cues, and possesses the necessary components in his behavioral experience which can be combined to reproduce the more complex, currently modeled behavior.

Imitative learning enables an individual to short-circuit the tedious and lengthy process of trial-and-error (or reward) learning while incorporating complex chains of behavior into his repertoire. Much of the behaviors which reflect the enduring part of our culture are to a large extent transmitted by repeated observation of behavior displayed by social models, particularly familial models. If performed frequently enough and rewarded in turn with approval by others, the imitated behavior will become incorporated into the patient's behavioral repertoire. The principles of imitative learning have been exploited with clinical success by researchers working with autistic children [12], phobic youngsters [4], and mute, chronic psychotics [18]. How modeling can be used in family therapy will be illustrated in the cases cited below.

I will limit the scope of the case examples to couples and families; however, the same principles of learning apply to group therapy [11,17] and with some modification to individual psychotherapy [9]. Although learning theory has been associated in clinical psychiatry with its systematic and explicit application in the new behavior therapies, it should be emphasized that learning theory offers a generic and unitary explanation of the processes mediating change in all psychotherapies, including psychoanalytic ones [1,13].

Technique

Before getting to the case material, I would like to outline the main features of an application of behavior theory to family therapy. The three major areas of technical concern for the therapist are: (1) *creating and maintaining a positive therapeutic alliance*; (2) *making a behavioral analysis of the problem(s)*; and (3) *implementing the behavioral principles of reinforcement and modeling in the context of ongoing interpersonal interactions*.

Without the positive therapeutic alliance between the therapist and those he is helping, there can be little or no successful intervention. The working alliance is the lever which stimulates change. In learning terms, the positive relationship between therapist and patient(s) permits the therapist to serve as a social reinforcer and model; in other words, to build up adaptive behaviors and allow maladaptive behaviors to extinguish. The therapist is an effective reinforcer and model for the patients to the extent that the patients value him and hold him in high regard and warm esteem.

Clinicians have described the ingredients that go into this positive therapist–patient relationship in many different ways. Terminology varies with the "school" of psychotherapy to which the clinician adheres. Psychoanalysts have contributed notions such as "positive transference" and an alliance between the therapist and the patient's "observing ego." Reality therapists call for a trusting involvement with the patient. Some clinicians have termed it a "supportive relationship" implying sympathy, respect, and concern on the part of the therapist. Recent research has labeled the critical aspects of the therapist–client relationship: nonpossessive warmth, accurate empathy, and genuine concern [20]. Truax and his colleagues [20] have been able to successfully operationalize these concepts and to teach them to selected individuals. They have further shown that therapists high on these attributes are more successful in psychotherapy than those who are not. Whatever the labels, a necessary if not sufficient condition for therapeutic change in patients is a doctor–patient relationship that is infused with mutual respect, warmth, trust, and affection.

In my experience, these qualities of the therapeutic alliance can be developed through a period of initial evaluation of the patient or family. The early therapist–family contacts, proceeding during the first few interviews, offer an opportunity to the therapist to show unconditional warmth, acceptance, and concern for the clients and their problems.

Also during the first few sessions, while the therapeutic relationship is being established, the therapist must do his "diagnostic." In a learning approach to family therapy, the diagnostic consists of a *behavioral* or *functional analysis* of the problems. In making his behavioral analysis, the therapist, in collaboration with the family, asks two major questions:

1. What behavior is maladaptive or problematic—what behavior in the designated patient should be increased or decreased? Each person, in turn, is asked, (1) what changes would you like to see in others in the family, and (2) how would you like to be different from the way you are now? Answering these questions forces the therapist to choose carefully *specific behavioral goals*.

2. What environmental and interpersonal contingencies currently support the problematic behavior—that is, what is maintaining undesirable behavior or reducing the likelihood of more adaptive responses? This is called a "functional analysis of behavior," and also can include an analysis of the development of symptomatic or maladaptive behavior, the "conditioning history" of the patient. The mutual patterns of social reinforcement in the family deserve special scrutiny in this analysis since their deciphering and clarification become central to an understanding of the case and to the formulation of therapeutic strategy.

It should be noted that the behavioral analysis of the problem doesn't end after the initial sessions, but by necessity continues throughout the course of therapy. As the problem behaviors change during treatment, so must the analysis of what maintains these behaviors. New sources of reinforcement for the patient and family members must be assessed. In this sense, the behavioral approach to family therapy is dynamic.

The third aspect of behavioral technique is the actual choice and implementation of therapeutic strategy and tactics. Which interpersonal transactions between the therapist and family members and among the family members can serve to alter the problem behavior in a more adaptive direction? The therapist acts as an educator, using his value as a social reinforcer to instruct the family or couple in changing their ways of dealing with each other. Some of the possible tactics are described in the case studies below.

A helpful way to conceptualize these tactics is to view them as "behavioral change experiments" where the therapist and family together re-program the contingencies of reinforcement operating in the family system. The behavioral

307

change experiments consists of family members responding to each other in various ways, with the responses contingent on more desired reciprocal ways of relating. Ballentine [2] views the behavioral change experiments, starting with small but well-defined successes, as leading to (1) a shift toward more optimistic and hopeful expectations; (2) an emphasis on doing things differently while giving the responsibility for change to each family member; (3) "encouragement of an observational outlook which forces family members to look closely at themselves and their relationships with one another, rather than looking 'inside' themselves with incessant why's and wherefores"; and (4) "the generation of empirical data which can be instrumental to further change, since they often expose sequences of family action and reaction in particularly graphic and unambiguous fashion."

The therapist also uses his importance as a model to illustrate desired modes of responding differentially to behavior that at times is maladaptive and at other times approaches more desirable form. The operant conditioning principle of "shaping" is used, whereby gradual approximations to the desired end behavior are reinforced with approval and spontaneous and genuine interest by the therapist. Through his instructions and example, the therapist teaches shaping to the members of the couple or family. Role playing or behavioral rehearsal are among the useful tactics employed in generating improved patterns of interaction among the family members.

The therapist using a behavioral model does not act like a teaching machine, devoid of emotional expression. Just as therapists using other theoretical schemas, he is most effective in his role as an educator when he expresses himself with affect in a comfortable, human style developed during his clinical training and in his life as a whole. Since intermittent reinforcement produces more durable behavior, the therapist may employ trial terminations, tapering off the frequency of sessions prior to termination and "booster" sessions [1]. The strategy and tactics of this behavioral approach to couples and families will be more clearly delineated in the case studies that follow. A more systematic and detailed outline of the behavior modification approach is presented in Table 1. The specification and implications of the items in this outline can be found in the manual by Reese [16].

Case 1

Mrs. D is a 35-year-old housewife and mother of three children who had a 15-year history of severe, migranous headaches. She had had frequent medical hospitalizations for her headaches (without any organic problems being found), and also a 1½-year period of intensive, psychodynamically oriented, individual psychotherapy. She found relief from her headaches only after retreating to her bed for periods of days to a week with the use of narcotics.

Table 1. A Behavioral Model for Learning

(Adapted from E. P. Reese[16])

---

1. Specify the final performance (therapeutic goals):
   Identify the behavior.
   Determine how it is to be measured.
2. Determine the current baseline rate of the desired behavior.
3. Structure a favorable situation for eliciting the desired behavior by providing cues for the appropriate behavior and removing cues for incompatible, inappropriate behavior.
4. Establish motivation by locating reinforcers, depriving the individual of reinforcers (if necessary), and withholding reinforcers for inappropriate behavior.
5. Enable the individual to become comfortable in the therapeutic setting and to become familiar with the reinforcers.
6. Shape the desired behavior:
   Reinforce successive approximations of the therapeutic goals.
   Raise the criterion for reinforcement gradually.
   Present reinforcement immediately, contingent upon the behavior.
7. Fade out the specific cues in the therapeutic setting to promote generalization of acquired behavior.
8. Reinforce intermittently to facilitate durability of the gains.
9. Keep continuous, objective records.

After a brief period of evaluation by me, she again developed intractable headaches and was hospitalized. A full neurological workup revealed no neuropathology. At this time I recommended that I continue with the patient and her husband in couple therapy. It had previously become clear to me that the patient's headaches were serving an important purpose in the economy of her marital relationship: Headaches and the resultant debilitation were the sure way the patient could elicit and maintain her husband's concern and interest in her. On his part, her husband was an active, action-oriented man who found it difficult to sit down and engage in conversation. He came home from work, read the newspaper, tinkered with his car, made repairs on the house, or watched TV. Mrs. D got her husband's clear-cut attention only when she developed headaches, stopped functioning as mother and wife, and took to her bed. At these times Mr. D was very solicitous and caring. He gave her medication, stayed home to take care of the children, and called the doctor.

My analysis of the situation led me to the strategy of redirecting Mr. D's attention to the adaptive strivings and the maternal and wifely behavior of his wife. During ten 45-minute sessions, I shared my analysis of the problem with Mr. and Mrs. D and encouraged them to reciprocally restructure their marital relationship. Once involved in a trusting and confident relationship with me, Mr. D worked hard to give his wife attention and approval for her day-to-day efforts as a mother and housewife. When he came home from work, instead of burying himself in the newspaper he inquired about the day at home and discussed with his wife problems concerning the children. He occasionally rewarded his wife's homemaking efforts by taking her out to a movie or to dinner (something they had not done for years). While watching TV he had his wife sit close to him or on his lap. In return, Mrs. D was taught to reward her husband's new efforts at intimacy with affection and appreciation. She let him know how much she liked to talk with him about the day's events. She prepared special dishes for him and kissed him warmly when he took initiative in expressing affection toward her. On the other hand, Mr. D was instructed to pay minimal attention to his wife's headaches. He was reassured that in so doing, he would be helping her decrease their frequency and severity. He was no longer to give her medication, cater to her when she was ill, or call the doctor for her. If she got a headache, she was to help herself and he was to carry on with his regular routine insofar as possible. I emphasized that *he should not, overall, decrease his attentiveness to his wife, but rather change the timing and direction of his attentiveness.* Thus the behavioral contingencies of Mr. D's attention changed from headaches to housework, from invalidism to active coping and functioning as mother and wife.

Within ten sessions, both were seriously immersed in this new approach toward each other. Their marriage was different and more satisfying to both. Their sex life improved. Their children were better behaved, as they quickly learned to apply the same reinforcement principles in reacting to the children and to reach a consensus in responding to their children's limit-testing. Mrs. D got a job as a department store clerk (a job she enjoyed and which provided her with further reinforcement—money and attention from people for "healthy" behavior). She was given recognition by her husband for her efforts to collaborate in improving the family's financial condition. She still had headaches, but they were mild and short-lived and she took care of them herself. Everyone was happier including Mrs. D's internist who no longer was receiving emergency calls from her husband.

A followup call to Mr. and Mrs. D one year later found them maintaining their progress. She has occasional headaches but has not had to retreat to bed or enter a hospital.

Case 2

Mrs. S is a 34-year-old mother of five who herself came from a family of ten siblings. She wanted very badly to equal her mother's output of children and also wanted to prove to her husband that he was potent and fertile. He had a congenital hypospadius and had been told by a physician prior to their marriage that he probably could not have children. Unfortunately Mrs. S was Rh negative and her husband Rh positive. After their fifth child she had a

310

series of spontaneous abortions because of the Rh incompatibility. Each was followed by a severe depression. Soon the depressions ran into each other and she was given a course of 150 EST's. The EST's had the effect of making her confused and unable to function at home while not significantly lifting the depressions. She had some successful short-term supportive psychotherapy but again plunged into a depression after a hysterectomy.

Her husband, like Mr. D in the previous case, found it hard to tolerate his wife's conversation, especially since it was taken up mostly by complaints and tearfulness. He escaped from the unhappy home situation by plunging himself into his work, holding two jobs simultaneously. When he was home, he was too tired for any conversation or meaningful interaction with his wife. Their sexual interaction was nil. Although Mrs. S tried hard to maintain her household and raise her children and even hold a part-time job, she received little acknowledgment for her efforts from her husband who became more distant and peripheral as the years went by.

My behavioral analysis pointed to a lack of reinforcement from Mrs. S's husband for her adaptive strivings. Consequently her depressions, with their large hypochondriacal components, represented her desperate attempt to elicit her husband's attention and concern. Although her somatic complaints and self-depreciating accusations were aversive for her husband, the only way he knew how to "turn them off" was to offer sympathy, reassure her of his devotion to her, and occasionally stay home from work. Naturally, his nurturing her in this manner had the effect of reinforcing the very behavior he was trying to terminate.

During five half-hour couple sessions I focused primarily on Mr. S, who was the mediating agent of reinforcement for his wife and hence the person who could potentially modify her behavior. I actively redirected his attention from his wife "the unhappy, depressed woman" to his wife "the coping woman." I forthrightly recommended to him that he drop his extra job, at least for the time being, in order to be at home in the evening to converse with his wife about the day's events, especially her approximations at successful home-making. I showed by my own example (modeling) how to support his wife in her efforts to assert herself reasonably with her intrusive mother-in-law and an obnoxious neighbor.

A turning point came after the second session, when I received a desperate phone call from Mr. S one evening. He told me that his wife had called from her job and tearfully complained that she could not go on and that he must come and bring her home. He asked me what he should do. I indicated that this was a crucial moment, that he should call her back and briefly acknowledge her distress but at the same time emphasize the importance of her finishing the evening's work. I further suggested that he meet her as usual after work and take her out for an ice cream soda. This would get across to her his abiding interest and recognition for her positive efforts in a genuine and spontaneous way. With this support from me, he followed my suggestions and within two weeks Mrs. S's depression had completely lifted.

She was shortly thereafter given a job promotion, which served as an extrinsic reinforcement for her improved work performance and was the occasion for additional reinforcement from me and her husband during the next therapy session. We terminated after the fifth session, a time limit we had initially agreed on.

Eight months later at followup they reported being "happier together than ever before."

Case 3

Edward is a 23-year-old young man who had received much psychotherapy, special schooling, and occupational counseling and training during the past 17 years. He was diagnosed at different times as a childhood schizophrenic and as mentally subnormal. At age 6 he was evaluated by a child psychiatry clinic and given three years of psychodynamic therapy by a psychoanalyst. He had started many remedial programs and finished almost none of them. He, in fact, was a chronic failure—in schools as well as in jobs. His parents viewed him as slightly retarded despite his low normal intelligence on IQ tests. He was infantilized by his mother and largely ignored or criticized by his father. He was used by his mother, who was domineering and aggressive, as an ally against the weak and passive father. When I began seeing them in a family evaluation, Edward was in the process of failing in the most recent rehabilitation effort—an evening, adult high school.

The initial goals of the family treatment, then, were (1) to disengage Edward from the clasp of his protective mother, (2) to get his father to offer himself as a model and as a source of encouragement (reinforcement) for Edward's desires and efforts towards independence, (3) to structure Edward's life with occupational and social opportunities that he could not initiate on his own. Fortunately the Jewish Vocational Service in Boston offers an excellent rehabilitation program based on the same basic principles of learning that have been elucidated in this article. I referred Edward to it and at the same time introduced him to a social club for ex-mental patients which has a constant whirl of activities daily and on weekends.

During our weekly family sessions, I used modeling and role-playing to help Edward's parents positively reinforce his beginning efforts at the J.V.S. and the social club. After three months at the J.V.S., Edward secured a job and now after another seven months has a job tenure and membership in the union. He has been an active member of the social club and has gone on weekend trips with groups there—something he had never done before. He is

312

now "graduating" to another social club, a singles' group in a church, and has started action on getting his driver's license.

The family sessions were not easy or without occasional storms, usually generated by Edward's mother as she from time to time felt "left out." She needed my support and interest (reinforcement) in her problems as a hard-working and unappreciated mother at these times. Because of the positive therapeutic relationship cemented over a period of nine months, Edward's parents slowly began to be able to substitute positive reinforcement for his gradually improving efforts at work and play instead of the previous blanket criticism (also, paradoxically, a kind of social reinforcement) he had received from them for his failures. I encouraged the father to share openly with Edward his own experiences as a young man reaching for independence, thereby serving as a model for his son.

The parents needed constant reinforcement (approval) from me for trying out new ways of responding to Edward's behavior; for example, to eliminate the usual nagging of him to do his chores around the house (which only served to increase the lethargic slothful behavior which accrues from the attention) and to indicate instead pleasure when he mows the lawn even if he forgets to rake the grass and trim the hedge. They learned to give Edward approval when he takes the garbage out even if he doesn't do it "their" way. And they learned how to spend time listening to Edward pour out his enthusiasm for his job even if they feel he is a bit too exuberant.

Our family sessions were tapered to twice monthly and then to once a month. Termination went smoothly after one year of treatment.

Case 4

Mr. and Mrs. F have a long history of marital strife. There was a year-long separation early in their marriage and several attempts at marriage counseling lasting three years. Mr. F has paranoid trends which are reflected in his extreme sensitivity to any lack of affection or commitment toward him by his wife. He is very jealous of her close-knit relationship with her parents. Mrs. F is a disheveled and unorganized woman who has been unable to meet her husband's expectations for an orderly and accomplished homemaker or competent manager of their five children. Their marriage has been marked by frequent mutual accusations and depreciation, angry withdrawal and sullenness.

My strategy with this couple, whom I saw for 15 sessions, was to teach them to stop reinforcing each other with attention and emotionality for undesired behavior and to begin eliciting desired behavior in each other using the principle of *shaping*. Tactically, I structured the therapy sessions with an important "ground-rule": No criticism or harping were allowed and they were to spend the time telling each other what the other had done during the

313

past week that approached the desired behaviors. As they gave positive feedback to each other for approximations to the behavior each valued in the other, I served as an auxiliary source of positive acknowledgment, reinforcing the reinforcer.

We began by clearly delineating what specific behaviors were desired by each of them in the other and by my giving them homework assignments in making gradual efforts to approximate the behavioral goals. For instance, Mr. F incessantly complained about his wife's lack of care in handling the evening meal—the disarray of the table setting, lack of tablecloth, disorderly clearing of the dishes. Mrs. F grudgingly agreed that there was room for improvement and I instructed her to make a start by using a tablecloth nightly. Mr. F in turn was told the importance of his giving her positive and consistent attention for her effort, since this was important to him. After one week they reported that they had been able to fulfill the assignment and that the evening meal was more enjoyable. Mrs. F had increased her performance to the complete satisfaction of her husband, who meanwhile had continued to give her positive support for her progress.

A similar process occurred in another problem area. Mr. F felt that his wife should do more sewing (mending clothes, putting on missing buttons) and should iron his shirts (which he had always done himself). Mrs. F was fed up with the home they lived in, which was much too small for their expanded family. Mr. F resolutely refused to consider moving to larger quarters because he felt it would not affect the quality of his wife's homemaking performance. I instructed Mrs. F to begin to do more sewing and ironing and Mr. F to reinforce this by starting to consider moving to a new home. He was to concretize this by spending part of each Sunday reviewing the real estate section of the newspaper with his wife and to make visits to homes that were advertised for sale. He was to make clear to her that his interest in a new home was *contingent* upon her improvements as a homemaker.

Between the third and sixth sessions, Mrs. F's father—who was ill with terminal lung cancer—was admitted to the hospital and died. During this period, we emphasized the importance of Mr. F giving his wife solace and support. I positively reinforced Mr. F's efforts in this direction. He was able to help his wife over her period of sadness and mourning despite his long-standing antagonism toward her father. Mrs. F in turn, with my encouragement, responded to her husband's sympathetic behavior with affection and appreciation. Although far from having an idyllic marriage, Mr. and Mrs. F have made tangible gains in moving closer toward each other.

Discussion

There is too much confusion in the rationales and techniques underlying current practices in family therapy. Although attempts to convey the method of family therapy always suffer when done through the written word, I do not share the belief that "the vital communications in all forms of psychotherapy are intuitive, felt, unspoken, and unconscious [7]." Although this article is not meant as a "how to do it" treatise for family therapists, I do intend it as a preliminary attempt to apply a few of the basic principles of imitative learning and operant conditioning to couple and family therapy.

Although the rationalized conceptualization of family therapy practiced by psychoanalytically oriented therapists differs from the learning and behavioral approach described here, closer examination of the actual techniques used reveals marked similarity. For example Framo [7], in explaining the theory behind his family therapy, writes:

> The overriding goal of the intensive middle phases consists in understanding and working through, often through transference to each other and to the therapists, the introjects of the parents so that the parents can see and experience how those difficulties manifested in the present family system have emerged from their unconscious attempts to perpetrate or master old conflicts arising from their families of origin. . . . The essence of the true work of family therapy is in the tracing of the vicissitudes of early object-relationships, and . . . the exceedingly intricate transformations which occur as a function of the intrapsychic and transactional blending of the old and new family systems of the parents. . . .

Despite the use of psychoanalytic constructs, Framo describes the actual process of family therapy in ways that are very compatible within a learning framework. He writes:

> Those techniques which prompt family interaction are the most productive in the long run. . . . It is especially useful to concentrate on here-and-now feelings; this method usually penetrated much deeper than dealing with feelings described in retrospect. . . . As we gained experience in working with families we became less hesitant about taking more forceful, active positions in order to help the family become unshackled from their rigid patterns.

Framo goes on to give illustrations of his work with families in which differential reinforcement for behavior considered more desirable and appropriate is given by the therapists. In dealing with angry and aggressive mothers, "we learned to avoid noticing what they did (e.g. emotional in-fighting) and pay attention to what they missed in life." Trying to activate passive fathers, "the therapists make every conscious effort to build him up during the sessions. . . . A number of techniques have been tried: Forcing more interaction between the husband and wife; assigning tasks; having a female therapist give encouragement in a flattering way; occasional individual sessions with the father." Zuk [23] describes his technique of family therapy in ways that fit into a reinforcement framework. He views the cornerstone of the technique the exploration and attempt "to shift the balance of pathogenic relation among family members so that new forms of relating become possible." Zuk further delineates the therapist's tactics as a "go-between" in which he uses his leverage to "constantly structure and direct the treatment situation."

It should be emphasized that the behavioral approach does not simplistically reduce the family system and family interaction to individualistic or dyadic mechanisms of reinforcement. The richness and complexity of family interaction is appreciated by the family therapist working within a behavioral framework. For instance, Ballentine [2] states:

> . . . behavior within a system cannot be so easily modified by focusing on the behavioral contingencies existing within any two-person subsystem, since one person's behavior in relation to a second's is often determined by behaviors of others within the system . . . the behavioral contingencies within a family system are manifold and constitute a matrix of multiple behavioral contingencies.

The complexity of family contingencies is exemplified by a transient problem which arose in Case 3. As Edward developed more independence from his parents and spent less and less time at home, his parents began to argue more angrily. Edward had served as a buffer between them—taking sides, being used as a scapegoat for their hostility, and serving as a "problem child" who required joint parental action and solidarity. With their buffer gone, the husband–wife relationship intensified and friction developed. Since the therapeutic goals were limited to Edward's emancipation from his parents and since it seemed that the parents were sufficiently symbiotic to contain a temporary eruption of hostility, the therapist's major efforts at this point were aimed at protecting Edward from backsliding in response to guilt or family pressure. The strategy worked, and within a few weeks the parents had reached a new modus vivendi with each other while Edward continued to consolidate and extend his gains.

A behavioral and learning approach to family therapy differs from a more psychoanalytic one. The therapist defines his role as an educator in collaboration with the family; therefore, the assigning of "sickness" labels to members, with its potential for moral blame, does not occur as it does under the medical model embodied in the psychoanalytic concept of underlying conflict or disease. There is no need for family members to acknowledge publicly their "weaknesses" or irrationality since insight per se is not considered vital.

The behavioral approach, with its more systematic and specific guidelines, makes it less likely that a therapist will adventitiously reinforce or model contradictory behavior patterns. The behavioral approach, consistently applied, is potentially more effective and faster. When patients do not respond to behavioral techniques, the therapist can use his more empirical attitude to ask why and perhaps to try another technique. The orientation is more experimental and "the patient is always right," with the burden on the therapist to devise effective interventions. In the psychoanalytic approach, the tendency has been for the therapist to decide that their failures are caused by patients who were inappropriate for the technique rather than viewing the technique as needing modification for the particular patient.

The work of behaviorally oriented family therapists is not restricted to the here-and-now of the therapy sessions. As the cases described reveal, much of the effort involves collaboration and involvement with adjunctive agencies such as schools, rehabilitation services, medication, and work settings. Family therapists are moving toward this total systems approach.

The advantages of behavioral approaches to family therapy sketched in this paper remain to be proven by systematic research. Such research is now proceeding [5,10,15,22]. Much work will go into demonstrating that family processes are "essentially behavioral sequences which can be sorted out, specified and measured with a fair degree of accuracy and precision [2]." Hopefully, further clinical and research progress made by behaviorally oriented therapists will challenge all family therapists, regardless of theoretical leanings, to specify more clearly their interventions, their goals, and their empirical results. If these challenges are accepted seriously, the field of family therapy will likely improve and gain stature as a scientifically grounded modality.

References

1. Alexander, F., 1965. The dynamics of psychotherapy in the light of learning theory. *Internat. J. Psychiat.*, **1**, 189–207.
2. Ballentine, R., 1968. The family therapist as a behavioral systems engineer . . . and a responsible one. Paper read at Georgetown Univ. Symp. on Fam. Psychother. Washington.
3. Bandura, A., and Walters, R., 1963. Social Learning and Personality Development. Holt, Rinehart and Winston, New York.
4. Bandura, A., Grusec, J., and Menlove, F., 1967. Vicarious extinction of avoidance behavior. *Personality and Soc. Psychol.* **5**, 16–23.
5. Dunham, R., 1966. Ex post facto reconstruction of conditioning schedules in family interaction. In *Family Structure, Dynamics and Therapy*, Irvin M. Cohen (Ed.), 107–114. Psychiatric Research No. 20, Amer. Psychiat. Assn., Washington.
6. Ferster, C., 1963. Essentials of a science of behavior. In *An Introduction to the Science of Human Behavior*, J. I. Nurnberger, C. B. Ferster, and J. P. Brady (Eds.), Appleton-Century-Crofts, New York.
7. Framo, J., 1965. Rationale and techniques of intensive family therapy. In *Intensive Family Therapy*, I. Boszormenyi-Nagy, and J. L. Framo (Eds.). Hoeber Medical Division, New York.
8. Handel, G. (Ed.), 1967. The Psychosocial Interior of the Family. Aldine, Chicago.
9. Krasner, L., 1962. The therapist as a social reinforcement machine. In *Research in Psychotherapy*, H. Strupp, and L. Luborsky (Eds.). Amer. Psychol. Assn., Washington.
10. Lewinsohn, P., Weinstein, M., and Shaw, D., 1969. Depression: A clinical research approach. In *Proceedings, 1968 Conference*, Assn. Advan. Behav. Ther., San Francisco. In press.
11. Liberman, R., 1970. A behavioral approach to group dynamics. *Behav. Ther.* In press.

12. Lovaas, O., *et al.*, 1966. Acquisition of imitative speech by schizophrenic children. *Science*, **151**, 705–707.
13. Marmor, J., 1966. Theories of learning and psychotherapeutic process. *Brit. J. Psychiat.*, **112**, 363–366.
14. Patterson G., *et al.*, 1967. Reprogramming the social environment. *Child Psychol. and Psychiat.* **8**, 181–195.
15. Patterson, G., and Reid, J., 1967. Reciprocity and coercion: Two facets of social systems. Paper read at 9th Ann. Inst. for Res. in Clin. Psychol. Univ. of Kansas.
16. Reese, E., 1966. The Analysis of Human Operant Behavior. Wm. C. Brown, Dubuque, Iowa.
17. Shapiro, D., and Birk, L., 1967. Group therapy in experimental perspectives. *Internat. J. Group Psychother.*, **17**, 211–224.
18. Sherman, J., 1965. Use of reinforcement and imitation to reinstate verbal behavior in mute psychotics. *J. Abnorm. Psychol.* **70**, 155–164.
19. Skinner, B., 1953. Science and Human Behavior. Macmillan, New York.
20. Truax, C., and Carkhuff, R., 1967. Toward Effective Counseling and Psychotherapy: Training and Practice. Aldine, Chicago.
21. Vogel, E., and Bell, N., 1960. The emotionally disturbed child as the family scapegoat. In *A Modern Introduction to the Family*, N. W. Bell and E. F. Vogel (Eds.). Free Press, New York.
22. Zeilberger, J., Sampen, S., and Sloane, H., 1968. Modification of a child's problem behaviors in the home with the mother as therapist. *J. Appl. Behav. Anal.* **1**, 47–53.
23. Zuk, G., 1967. Family therapy. *Arch. Gen. Psychiat.*, **16**, 71–79.

REFERENCES

Ayllon, T. Intensive Treatment of Psychotic Behavior by Stimulus Satiation and Food Reinforcement. *Behavior Research and Therapy*, 1963, **1**, 53–62.

Ayllon, T., Azrin, N. H. *The token economy*. New York: Appleton-Century-Crofts, 1968.

Bandura, A., *Principles of behavior modification*. New York: Holt, Rinehart, & Winston, 1969.

Birk, C. L. Combined Aversive Conditioning and Group Psychotherapy for Homosexuals. Unpublished Manuscript, 1969.

Bond, I. K., & Evans, D. R. Avoidance Therapy: Its Use in Two Cases of Underwear Fetishism. *Canadian Medical Association Journal*, 1967, **96**, 1160–1162.

Cohen, H., Fillipczak, J., & Bis, J. S. *Case I: An initial study of contingencies applicable to special education*. Silver Spring, Md.: Educational Facility Press, 1967.

Colman, A., & Baker, S. Utilization of an Operant Conditioning Model for the Treatment of Character and Behavior Disorders in a Military Setting. *Amer. J. Psychiat.*, 1969, **125**, 1395–1403.

Darwin, C. *The expression of the emotions in man and animals*. New York: Appleton, 1896.

Ferster, C. B. Essentials of a Science of Behavior, in *An introduction to the science of human behavior* by Nurnberger, Ferster and Brady. New York: Appleton-Century-Crofts, 1963, pp. 199–345.

Ferster, C. B., & Simons, J. Behavior Therapy with Children. *Psychological Record*, 1966, **16**, 65–71.

Freud, S. Further Recommendations on the Technique of Psychoanalysis, in *Collected papers*, Vol. II, p. 342. London: Hogarth Press, 1948.

Freud, S. Fragment of an Analysis of a Case of Hysteria, in *Collected papers*, Vol. III, pp. 13–148. New York: Basic Books, 1959a.

Freud, S. On Psychotherapy, in *Collected papers*, Vol. I, pp. 251–256. New York: Basic Books, 1959b.

Friedman, P. H. The Effects of Modeling and Roleplaying on Assertive Behavior, in R. Rubin (Ed.), *Advances in behavior therapy*, Volume II. New York: Academic Press, 1970.

Gericke, O. L. Practical Use of Operant Conditioning Procedures in a Mental Hospital, *Psychiatric Studies and Projects*, American Psychiatric Association, Volume III, No. 5, June 1965.

Goldiamond, I. Fluent and Nonfluent Speech (Stuttering): Analysis and Operant Techniques for Control. In L. Krasner and L. P. Ullmann (Eds.), *Research in behavior modification*. New York: Holt, Rinehart, & Winston, 1965. pp. 106–156.

Graubard, P. S., Miller, S. U., & Weisert, H. "Behavior Modification, Group Process and Attitudes of Group Members." Paper presented to Annual Meeting of American Orthopsychiatric Association, New York, March 1969.

Harris, F., Johnston, M., Kelley, S., & Wolf, M. M. Effects of Positive Social Reinforcement on Regressed Crawling of a Nursery School Child. *J. Educational Psychology*, 1964, **55**, 35–41.

Heckel, R. B., Wiggins, S. L., & Salzberg, H. C. Conditioning Against Silences in Group Therapy. *J. Clin. Psychol.*, 1962, **18**, 216–217.

Heine, R. W. A Comparison of Patients' Reports on Psychotherapeutic Experiences with Psychoanalytic, Nondirective, and Adlerian Therapists. *Amer. J. Psychother.* 1953, **7**, 16–23.

Hingtgen, J. N., Coulter, S. K., & Churchill, D. W. Intensive Reinforcement of Imitative Behavior in Mute Autistic Children. Unpublished Manuscript, Indiana University Medical Center, 1967.

Homme, L., *et al. How to use contingency contracting in the classroom.* Champaign, Ill.: Research Press, 1969.

Isaacs, W., Thomas, J., & Goldiamond, I. Application of Operant Conditioning to Reinstate Verbal Behavior in Psychotics. *J. Speech and Hearing Disorders*, 1960, **25**, 8–12.

Jacobson, S., Lewinsohn, P. N., & Flippo, J. F. An Application of the Premack Principle to the Verbal Behavior of Depressed Subjects in Advances, in R. Rubin (Ed.), *Behavior Therapy.* New York: Academic Press, 1970.

Jones, M. C. The Elimination of Children's Fears. *J. Exp. Psychol.*, 1924, **7**, 383–390.

Lent, J. R. Mimosa Cottage: Experiment in Hope. *Psychology Today*, 1968, **2**, 51–58.

Lewinsohn, P. M., Weinstein, M., & Shaw, D. Depression: A Clinical-Research Approach, in R. Rubin (Ed.), *Advances in behavior therapy.* New York: Academic Press, 1969, pp. 231–240.

Liberman, R. P. A View of Behavior Modification Projects in California. *Behavior Research and Therapy*, 1968, **6**, 331–341.

Liberman, R. P. A Behavioral Approach to Group Dynamics. *Behavior Therapy*, 1970, **1**, 141–175 and 312–327.

Liberman, R. P., & Raskin, D. F. Depression: A behavioral formulation. *Arch. General Psychiat.* 1971. In Press.

Lovaas, O. I. A Behavior Therapy Approach to the Treatment of Childhood Schizophrenia, in J. P. Hill (Ed.), *Minnesota symposium on child psychology*, Volume I, pp. 108–159. Minneapolis: University of Minnesota Press, 1967.

Madsen, C. *Teaching discipline.* Boston: Allyn & Bacon, 1970.

Madsen, C. H., Jr., Becker, W. C., & Thomas, D. R. Rules, Praise, and Ignoring: Elements of Elementary Classroom Control. *Journal Applied Behavior Analysis*, 1968, **1**, 139–150.

Marks, I. M., Boulongouris, J. C., & Marset, P. "Flooding (Implosion) vs. Desensitization in Phobias." Scientific Proceedings of Amer. Psychiat. Assn. Annual Meeting, San Francisco, May 1970. pp. 241–242.

Marmor, J. Theories of Learning and the Psychotherapeutic Process. *British J. Psychiatry*, 1966, **112**, 363–366.

Metz, J. R. Operant Conditioning in Behavior Therapy: Some Illustrations and Reflections. *California Mental Health Research Symposium No. 2*, 1968.

Moser, D. Screams, Slaps and Love. *Life*, May 7, 1965, pp. 90A–101.

O'Leary, K. D., Becker, W. C., Evans, M. B., & Saudargas, R. A. A Token Reinforcement Program in a Public School: A Replication and Systematic Analysis. *Journal Applied Behavior Analysis*, 1969, **2**, 3–14.

Patterson, G. R., & Gullion, M. E. *Living with children: New methods for parents and teachers.* Champaign, Ill.: Research Press, 1968.

Patterson, G. R., & Reid, J. "Reciprocity and Coercion: Two Facets of Social Systems," Paper read at the Ninth Annual Institute for Research in Clinical Psychology, University of Kansas, April, 1967.

Premack, D. Toward Empirical Behavior Laws: I. Positive Reinforcement. *Journal of Psychological Review*, 1959, **23**, 219–233.

Raymond, J. J. The Treatment of Addiction by Aversion Conditioning with Apomorphine. *Behav. Res. and Therapy*, 1964, **1**, 287–291.

Reich, W. *Character analysis.* New York: Noonday Press, Farrer, Straus & Giroux, 1949.

Rogers, C. Some Issues Concerning the Control of Human Behavior: A Symposium. *Science*, 1956, **124**, 1057–1066.

Rosenthal, D. Changes in Some Moral Values Following Psychotherapy. *Journal of Consulting Psychology*, 1955, **19**, 431–436.

Schaefer, H., & Martin, P. *Behavioral therapy*, New York: McGraw-Hill, 1969.

Schwitzgebel, R. *Street corner research*. Cambridge: Harvard Univ. Press, 1966.

Shelton, J. T. "The Use of Operant Conditioning With Disturbed Adolescent, Retarded Boys." Paper delivered at Twentieth Mental Hospital Institute, Washington, D.C., 1968.

Skinner, B. F. *Science and human behavior*. New York: Macmillan, 1953.

Smith, J. M., & Smith, D. E. P. *Child management: A program for parents*. Ann Arbor, Mich.: Ann Arbor Publishers, 1966.

Stampfl, T. G., & Levis, D. J. Implosive Therapy—A Behavioral Therapy? *Behavior, Research and Therapy*, 1968, **6**, 31–36.

Storrow, H. A., & Spanner, M. Does Psychotherapy Change Patient's Attitudes? *J. Nervous Mental Disease*, 1962, **134**, 440.

Sylvester, J. D., & Liversedge, L. A. Conditioning and the Occupational Cramps, in H. J. Eysenck (Ed.), *Behavior therapy and the neuroses*. Oxford: Pergamon Press, 1960, pp. 334–348.

Thomas, D. R., Becker, W. C., & Armstrong, M. Production and Elimination of Disruptive Classroom Behavior by Systematically Varying Teacher's Behavior. *Journal Applied Behavioral Analysis*, 1968, **1**, 35–45.

Ullmann, L., & Krasner, L. (Eds.), *Case Studies in behavior modification*. New York: Holt, Rinehart, & Winston, 1965.

Walder, L. O. "Teaching Parents to Modify the Behaviors of Their Autistic Children." Paper read at American Psychological Association, New York, September 1966.

Walton, D. The Application of Learning Theory to the Treatment of a Case of Neurodermatitis, in H. J. Eysenck (Ed.), *Behavior Therapy and the Neuroses*. New York: Pergamon Press, 1960, pp. 272–274.

Williams, C. D. The Elimination of Tantrum Behavior by Extinction Procedures. *Journal of Abnormal and Social Psychology*, 1959, **59**, 269.

Wolpe, J. *Psychotherapy by Reciprocal Inhibition*. Stanford: Stanford University Press, 1958.

Wolpe, J. *The practice of behavior therapy*. New York: Pergamon Press, 1969.

Wolpe, J., & Lazarus, A. A. *Behavior therapy techniques*. New York: Pergamon Press, 1966.

A Selected, Annotated Bibliography on Behavior Modification

Prepared by:
Daniel G. Brown, Ph.D.
Consultant in Mental Health
National Institute of Mental Health
Southeast Regional Office
Atlanta, Georgia 30323

This Bibliography is primarily concerned with applications of behavioral analysis modification, operant conditioning, and behavior therapy to a wide range of human conditions and mental health problems. Its purpose is to provide a basic list of references of particular interest and value to mental health and mental health-related personnel working in a variety of institutional, community, school and clinic settings.

Atthowe, J. M., Jr., & Krasner, L. A. Preliminary Report on the Application of Contingent Reinforcement Procedures (Token Economy) on a "Chronic" Psychiatric Ward. *Journal of Abnormal Psychology*, 1968, **73**, 37–43.

> Report of two-year study of 86-bed closed ward, token economy, operant conditioning project in a Veterans Administration Hospital involving chronic schizophrenic and brain damaged patients. The token contingency program was successful in combating institutionalism and in increasing initiative, responsibility and social interaction in these patients. It was concluded that this approach can be an important adjunct to any rehabilitation effort concerned with chronic or apathetic patients.

Ayllon, T., & Azrin, N. H. *Token economy: A motivational system for therapy and rehabilitation.* New York: Appleton-Century-Crofts, 1969.

> A review and discussion of various research projects concerned with the application of operant procedures to patients in mental hospitals. Based on the pioneer work of the authors with institutionalized patients over the past ten years and includes a connected with token-economy and related operant procedures with inpatient populations. 116 References.

Bandura, A. Behavioral Psychotherapy. *Scientific American.* March 1967, **216**, 78–86.

> Presents a brief, relatively non-technical discussion of the rationale of behavior modification and various approaches in behavior therapy and modeling techniques as applied to cases of stuttering, childhood schizophrenia, hyperactive behavior, fears and phobias, delinquency, etc.

Bandura, A. *Principles of behavior modification.* New York: Holt, Rinehart, & Winston, 1969.

> Discusses recent developments in behavior modification in terms of principles, theory, research and applications. Extended discussions are included of positive and negative reinforcement, extinction, desensitization, and aversive counter conditioning. The distinctive emphasis of this volume is on cognitive, vicarious. modeling and self-mediating processes. Symbolic controls, conscious and unconscious awareness, attitudes, self-regulatory functions, etc., are discussed in terms of behavioral changes.

Becker, W. C., Thomas, D. R., & Carnine, D. Applications of Operant Conditioning Principles in Reducing Behavior Problems in the Elementary School: A State of the Art Review for Teachers. Pre-publication paper, 1969. (Available from Dr. Wesley C. Becker, Bureau of Educational Research, University of Illinois. Education Building, Urbana, Illinois 61801.)

> This material was written particularly for teachers and other adults who work with children in group settings. It summarizes a considerable amount of recent work involving the use of behavior modification in decreasing disruptive and other deviant behaviors and in increasing desirable behavior in children. Concepts, principles, and procedures of operant-reinforcement learning are clearly set forth and discussed in terms of application to pre-school and school-age children.

Bernal, M. E. Behavioral Feedback in the Modification of Brat Behaviors, *J. Nerv. Mental Disease*, 1969, **148**, 375–385.

An applied research program demonstrating the use of operant learning principles and behavioral feedback via television to train mothers in child management. Tailored programs for two male "brats" aged 5 and 8 years are presented. Seven instruction sessions were held during which the mothers' management behaviors were gradually shaped. According to daily notes kept by the mothers of the boys' disciplinary problems at home, both children improved markedly within a period of 25 weeks from the point of first contact.

Bricker, W. A. Introduction to Behavior Modification. Peabody Papers in Human Development, 1968. (Available from Dr. William A. Bricker, Department of Psychology, George Peabody College for Teachers, Nashville, Tennessee 37203).

Covers basic principles of behavior modification and relates them to a number of adults and children with a variety of deviant behaviors that were effectively modified.

Brown, D. G. Behavior Modification with Children. Pre-publication paper, 1969. (Available from Dr. Daniel G. Brown, N.I.M.H. Regional Office, Room 404, 50 Seventh Street, N.E., Atlanta, Georgia 30323.)

Brief overview of developments in behavior modification in relation to children and youth, including basic concepts and procedures, advantages, application to various deviant behaviors, criticisms and resistances to behavior modification, manpower implications, etc.

Burchard, J., & Tyler, V., Jr. The Modification of Delinquent Behavior through Operant Conditioning. *Behaviour Research and Therapy*, 1965, **2**, 245–250.

Case of 13-year-old male delinquent who responded to operant conditioning with decreased anti-social behavior and decreased seriousness of offenses; the operant approach over a five-month period was more effective than psychotherapy used during previous four years of institutionalization.

Clos, M. C. "Behavior Modification Treatment in a Day Hospital." Paper presented at the Annual Meeting of the American Psychological Association, Washington, D.C., 1967. (Available from Dr. Marjorie C. Clos, Caro State Hospital, Caro, Michigan 48723.)

Describes the application and successful use of behavior modification in a day program in the New Orleans Regional Mental Health Center. The case of a 20-year-old female schizophrenic is used as an example of the effectiveness of a behavioral approach to patients in a day setting.

Eysenck, H. J. New Ways in Psychotherapy. *Psychology Today*, **1**, No. 2, June 1967, 39–47.

The author repeats his well known criticism of traditional approaches in psychotherapy and then reviews the rationale and principles of the behavior therapies including classical conditioning, reciprocal inhibition and desensitization, treatment machines, operant conditioning, etc.

Franks, C. M. (Ed.) *Behavior therapy: Appraisal and status.* New York: McGraw-Hill, 1969.

This is an up-to-date, systematic, and comprehensive overview of the field—covering technique, philosophy, social implications, and experimental bases. There are excellent reviews of systematic desensitization, behavior therapy with children, verbal conditioning, and behavioral diagnosis.

Gelfand, D. M., Gelfand, S., & Dobson, W. R. Unprogrammed Reinforcement of Patients Behavior in a Mental Hospital. *Behaviour Research and Therapy,* 1967, **5,** 201–207

Analysis of the reinforcements that psychotic patients typically receive in a mental hospital environment. Social and psychotic behaviors were inconsistently reinforced, with severely psychotic behavior being more inappropriately reinforced. Implications for training hospital staff, particularly nurses, are discussed.

Hall, R. V., Lund, D., & Jackson, D. Effects of Teacher Attention on Study Behavior. *Journal of Applied Behavior Analysis,* 1968, **1,** 1–12.

The effects of contingent teacher attention on study behavior were investigated. Individual rates of study were recorded for one first-grade and five third-grade pupils who had high rates of disruptive or dawdling behavior. A reinforcement period (in which teacher attention followed study behavior and non-study behaviors were ignored) resulted in sharply increased study rates. A brief reversal of the contingency (attention occurred only after periods of non-study behavior) again produced low rates of study. Reinstatement of teacher attention as reinforcement for study once again markedly increased study behavior. Follow-up observations indicated that the higher study rates were maintained after the formal program terminated.

Hall, R. V., Panyan, M., Rabon, D., & Broden, M. Instructing Beginning Teachers in Reinforcement Procedures which Improve Classroom Control. *J. Applied Behav. Anal.,* 1968, **1,** 315–322.

Reports on consultation to three beginning teachers (1st, 6th and 7th grades) who had experienced difficulty maintaining classroom control, teaching satisfactorily, etc. These teachers learned how to use systematic reinforcement procedures and were able to bring about marked improvements in class management, study behaviors in students, etc. The authors conclude that these behavior modification procedures "can be employed by teachers in any classroom without added expense and without major administrative revision, *now.*"

Hawkins, R. P., Peterson, R. F., Schweid, E., & Bijou, S. W. Behavior Therapy in the Home: Amelioration of Problem Parent-Child Relationships with the Parent in a Therapeutic Role, *Journal of Experimental Child Psychology,* 1967, **4,** 99–107.

The experimental modification of a problem mother-child relationship is described. The child, a 4-year-old boy, was extremely difficult to manage and control. Treatment was carried out in the home with the mother as therapist guided by a mental health professional. The child's objectionable behaviors were observed to change in frequency and quality as a consequence of the treatment and appeared to generalize from the experimental hours to the remaining hours of the day. Nearly a month later, these changes were still in evidence.

327

Homme, L. E. Contingency Management. *Educational Technology Monographs*. II, No. 2, 1969. (Available from Dr. Lloyd Homme, Research Department, Westinghouse Learning Corporation, Albuquerque, New Mexico 87106.)

A brief, practical discussion based on Premack's principle that for any pair of responses, the more probable one (e.g. playing at school) can be used to reinforce the less probable one (e.g. studying at school). Applications of this operant procedure are discussed in terms of pre-school, poverty, normal middle class, Indian, and retarded children, as well as to a blind adolescent in a state mental hospital.

Homme, L. E., Csanyi, A. P., Gonzales, M. A., & Rechs, J. R. *How to use contingency contracting in the classroom.* Champaign, Ill.: Research Press, 1969.

This "how-to-do-it" manual explains an extremely effective method of motivating elementary and high school students. The method, contingency contracting, involves an agreement between the teacher and his students under which rewards are promised in return for the desired learning behavior by the students.

Jacobson, J. M., Bushell, D., Jr., & Risley, T. Switching Requirements in a Head Start Classroom. *Journal of Applied Behavior Analysis*, 1969, **2**, 43–47.

Two experiments were conducted by the mothers of the children in a Head Start classroom. Both examined the effects of a switching task on the frequency with which children moved from one activity area of the classroom to another. The results indicated that the rate at which the children changed activities could be adjusted by varying the difficulty or magnitude of the switching task and that the task itself could be used to introduce academic subjects which would be poorly attended if initially presented in an activity area.

Krasner, L., & Ullmann, L. P. (Eds.) *Research in behavior modification.* New York: Holt, Rinehart, & Winston, 1965.

Fifteen original articles that: (1) Review major research areas in behavior modification; (2) focus on the application of experimental findings to the modification of a variety of clinical behaviors; and (3) discuss future developments of relevance to all mental health disciplines. 645 References.

Krumboltz, J. D. (Ed.) *Revolution in counseling: Implications of behavioral science.* New York: Houghton Mifflin, 1966.

This small volume of slightly more than 100 pages contains the major papers by Krumboltz, Bijou, Shoben, McDaniel and Wrenn, presented at a conference held at Stanford University in 1965. The term, "revolution," refers to the systematic application of behaviorism and, particularly, operant conditioning to the counseling process. Imitative learning or modeling, cognitive learning and emotional-classical conditioning are also discussed.

Krumboltz, J. D., & Thoresen, C. E. *Behavioral counseling.* New York: Holt, Rinehart, & Winston, 1969.

This book describes 43 promising counseling techniques that have been shown to benefit clients. Each technique is described in sufficient detail that another

328

counselor can duplicate the treatment upon reading the account. Methods involving reinforcement, social modeling, and cognitive learning are given prominence.

Layton, M. M. Behavior Therapy and its Implications for Psychiatric Nursing. *Perspectives In Psychiatric Care*, 1966, **4**, 38–52.

Discusses the history, present status and basic principles of behavior therapy including both Pavlovian and Operant conditioning approaches. Although written primarily for nurses, the material would also be of interest to other mental health personnel. See also D. G. Brown, Behavior Modification, *Perspectives in Psychiatric Care*, 1968, **6**, 224–229, a paper concerned with applications and implications for psychiatric-mental health nursing, maternal and child-health nursing and public health nursing.

Lazarus, A. A., Davison, G. C., & Polefka, D. A. Classical and Operant Factors in the Treatment of a School Phobia. *Journal of Abnormal Psychology*, 1965, **70**, 225–229.

Case of a nine-year-old boy whose avoidance behavior of school was: (1) Motivated by intense fear of school, and (2) maintained by various secondary reinforcements such as parental and peer attention, etc. Both classical (counter conditioning) and operant (reinforcement contingencies on school attendance) techniques were combined in the successful treatment of this case.

Leslie, G. R. (Ed.) *Behavior modification in rehabilitation facilities*. Hot Springs Rehabilitation Center, 1969. Hot Springs, Arkansas 71901.

An educational resource manual based on papers presented at a Seminar on Behavior Modification in Rehabilitation Facilities in 1968 for rehabilitative center executives and administrators.

Lewinsohn, P. M., Weinstein, M. S., & Shaw, D. A. Depression: A Clinical-Research Approach. *Advances in behavior therapy*, 1968. Edited by R. D. Rubin & C. M. Franks. New York: Academic Press, 1969, pp. 231–240.

Reports on the use of behavioral analysis in the treatment of depression. Depression is interpreted as a function of inadequate positive reinforcement in the person's present life, based on environmental deficits such as loss through death, poverty, misfortune, etc., and personal deficits such as lack of skill, ignorance, etc.; these deficits, in turn, produce a low rate of activity and verbal behavior plus social reinforcements in the form ot sympathy, concern, etc. Applications to several cases are discussed.

Liberman, R. A View of Behavior Modification Projects in California. *Behaviour Research and Therapy*, 1968, **6**, 331–341.

Descriptions of operant-reinforcement programs at seven facilities in California, including two with chronic schizophrenics (Patton State and Menlo Park V.A. Hospitals), two with adolescent-young adult retardates (Pacific and Sonoma State Hospitals), four with disturbed and retarded children (Sonoma and Pacific State Hospitals, UCLA Psychiatric Institute and Santa Clara Mental Health Center) and one with Job Corpsmen (Parks Job Corps Center).

Liberman, R. Behavioral Approaches to Family and Couple Therapy. *American Journal of Orthopsychiatry*, 1970, **40**, 106–118.

Discusses the application of behavior modification to marriage and family therapy; four cases are described in which behavioral analysis is effectively utilized. The key to successful couple or family therapy, whatever the theoretical positions of the therapists, can be found in the changes made in the interpersonal consequences of the members' behavior.

Liberman, R. A Behavioral Approach to Group Dynamics. *Behavior Therapy*, 1970, **1**, 141–175 and 312–327.

Two outpatient, nonpsychotic therapy groups were compared in terms of process and outcome. One group was led by a therapist who was "programmed" to reinforce and prompt cohesiveness and hostility-to-the-leader and the other group was led in an intuitive, group dynamic mode. The experimental group had much greater cohesiveness and its members showed greater personality changes in desired directions and faster symptomatic improvement than the comparison group. In both groups, evidence was obtained for viewing the therapist as a social reinforcer for group dynamic behaviors.

Lindsley, O. R. An Experiment with Parents Handling Behavior at Home. *Johnstone Bulletin*, 1966, **9**, 27–36 (Johnstone Training Center, Bordentown, New Jersey).

Reports on the author's work with group of fathers in the effective use of behavior modification with their retarded children in the home. Discusses the procedures used including the "Sunday Box" and the "Point Store." See also the author's pre-publication paper, Operant Behavior Management: Background and Procedures, which discusses Pavlovian and Operant conditioning and outlines the basic steps in behavior modification of pinpointing, recording, consequating and trying again. (Available from Dr. O. R. Lindsley, Bureau of Child Research), University of Kansas Medical Center, Kansas City, Kansas 66103.)

Lovaas, O. I. A Behavior Therapy Approach to the Treatment of Childhood Schizophrenia. In J. P. Hill (Ed.), *Minnesota symposia on child psychology*, Vol. 1. Minneapolis: University of Minnesota Press, 1967.

The author summarized his work utilizing behavior modification with severely psychotic children with particular emphasis on the development of speech. He discusses the rationale, previous developments and basic conceptualizations in reinforcement learning theory and therapy.

Madsen, C. H., Jr., & Madsen, C. K. *Teaching discipline behavioral principles toward a positive approach*. Boston: Allyn & Bacon, 1970.

A small volume of 139 pages "written especially for the teacher and prospective teacher . . . as a guide in the use of behavioral principles." A series of 20 questions and answers (e.g., What is behavior modification? Why don't students learn? etc.) and a selected sample of 55 scientific and professional examples of behavior changing practices applicable to classroom teaching situations (e.g. disruptive, out-of-control behaviors, boredom, apathy, low achievement and academic failures, nailbiting, non-cooperative and socially withdrawn behaviors, etc.).

Malott, R. W., & Whaley, D. L. *Elementary principles of behavior*, Vols. 1 and 2, Kalamazoo, Mich.: Department of Psychology, Western Michigan University, 1968.

These volumes were written as a comprehensive introduction to behavioral analysis and modification for college students, either as basic text or as a supplementary reference. Interestingly presented in a novel manner, this material contains discussions of all of the major principles and concepts in behavior modification together with case excerpts and illustrative applications from research work in the field.

Martin, M., Burkholder, R., Rosenthel, T. L., Tharp, R. G., & Thorne, G. L. Programming Behavior Change and Re-Integration into School Milieux of Extreme Adolescent Deviates. *Behaviour Research and Therapy*, 1968, **6**, 371–384.

Behavior-change programs for returning problem adolescents from an experimental school to regular classrooms were attempted. The use of contingent reinforcement and contracts with families are described.

Mertens, G., Luker, A., & Boltuck, C. *Behavioral science behaviorally taught*, Minneapolis: Burgess Publishing Company, 1968.

This book was written within an operant conditioning framework and designed as a "personalized text" for individuals interested in understanding the nature, principles, and applications of behavioral analysis and modification. The contents, which are contained in a loose leaf binder, consist of a combination of selected readings, reports, and excerpts from the professional literature, plus accompanying expository material by the authors along with exercises and texts for each selection. In addition to covering major operant principles, includes such topics as programmed teaching and learning, ethical issues, applications to psychotic patients, alcoholics, overeating, mental retardation, etc.

O'Leary, K. D., Becker, W. C., Evans, M. B., & Sandargas, R. A., A Token Reinforcement System in a Public School. *J. Applied Behav. Anal.*, 1969, **2**, 3–14.

Reports on the use of behavior modification with seven members of a second grade class who spent over half of their time in various disruptive, unproductive behaviors. Rules, praise, ignoring a point system and star system that could be exchanged for back-up reinforcements, etc., were carried out by the teacher with assistance from the consultant. The author concludes that a combined reinforcement and individualized programmed instruction system can provide an extremely effective learning environment particularly for "that large group of children who have not learned the value of learning."

O'Leary, K. D., O'Leary, S., & Becker, W. C. Modification of a Deviant Sibling Interaction Pattern in the Home. *Behaviour Research and Therapy*, 1967, **5**, 113–120.

Reports on the effective use of a token reinforcement and time-out from reinforcement procedure with a 6-year-old boy and his 3-year-old brother who frequently engaged in a variety of deviant behaviors including kicking, hitting, throwing things at each other, and other destructive acts. The treatment program was carried out in the home for several months and involved the parent (mother) learning to function as a therapist for these two brothers.

Patterson, G. R., & Bodsky, G. A. Behavior Modification Programme for a Child, *Journal of Child Psychology and Psychiatry*, 1966, **7**, 277–295.

Manipulation of reinforcement contingencies has a significant impact upon behavior. The major focus of the behavior modifier should be upon the task of directly manipulating the reinforcement being provided by the social environment, rather than upon the behavior of the individual subject.

Patterson, G. R., & Gullion, M. E. *Living with children: New methods for parents and teachers.* Champaign, Ill.: Research Press (Box 2459, Station A), 1968.

Written as a practical guide and programmed manual concerned with helping parents and teachers understand and learn how to modify various behaviors of children. Specific chapters outline the use of behavior modification with children who are: (1) Overly aggressive; (2) overly negativistic; (3) hyperactive; (4) over-dependent; (5) fearful; and (6) withdrawn. This material is based on the extensive experiences of the authors in carrying out applied research with parents and teachers.

Patterson, G. R., McNeal, S., Hawkins, N., & Phelps, R. Reprogramming the Social Environment. *Journal of Child Psychology and Psychiatry*, 1967, **8**, 181–195.

The hypothesis is presented that the behavior modifier should focus his efforts upon altering the social environment in which the child lives rather than directly upon the deviant child. Within such a framework, alterations in the reinforcement schedules being used by the parents, or the peer group, would produce changes in the behavior of the child.

Patterson, G. R., Ray, R. S., & Shaw, D. A. "Direct Intervention in Families of Deviant Children." Oregon Research Institute Bulletin, Vol. 8, No. 9, 1968 (Available from the authors at ORI, Eugene Oregon).

Data are presented from observations made for six children demonstrating the effect of direct intervention in home and school. Observations underline feasibility of training parents, siblings, peers and teachers to alter behavior of an identified deviant child.

Paul, G. L. Chronic Mental Patient: Current Status—Future Directions. *Psychological Bulletin*, 1969, **71**, 81–94.

The milieu therapy approach is contrasted with the token economy (behavioral) approach in the treatment and rehabilitation of chronic, long-term hospitalized patients. The need for specific supportive measures to assist the patient to remain in the community after discharge is highlighted by suggestions for future action.

Phillips, E. L. Achievement Place: Token Reinforcement Procedures in a Home-Style Rehabilitation Setting for "Pre-Delinquent" Boys. *J. Applied Behavior Analysis*, 1968, **3**, 213–224.

Points (tokens) were given by houseparents contingent upon specified appropriate behavior and taken away for specified inappropriate behavior. Points were redeemable by the boys ($N = 3$) for various privileges such as home visits, watching TV, and riding bicycles. The frequencies of aggressive statements and poor grammar decreased while tidiness, punctuality, and amount of homework completed increased. It was concluded that a token reinforcement procedure, entirely dependent upon back-up reinforcers naturally available in a home-style setting, could contribute to an effective and economical rehabilitation program for pre-delinquents.

Risley, T. R., & Wolf, M. M. Experimental Manipulation of Autistic Behaviors and Generalization into the Home, In S. W. Bijou and D. M. Baer (Eds.), *Child Development: Readings in experimental analysis.* New York: Appleton-Century-Crofts, 1967.

The case of a six-year-old autistic child is reported. Shows that the mothers of children who have behavior problems can be trained to deal effectively with the problem. In the instances reported in this paper, the problem is one of shaping discriminated verbal operants, a task involving both discrimination and differential contingencies. The method of training the parents includes demonstration, imitation by the parents, and reinforcement by the experimenters of correct imitations.

Schaefer, H. H., & Martin, P. L. *Behavioral therapy.* New York: McGraw-Hill, 1969.

Written as a training manual and handbook for mental health personnel engaged in carrying out behavior modification procedures in mental hospitals and other institutional settings. Covers the nature of mental illness, history of mental institutions, fundamentals of behavioral analysis, procedures and techniques, the behavioral programs at Patton State Hospital in California, ward management, modification of specific deviant behaviors such as delusions, hallucinations, mutism, crazy talk, manipulative acts, violent behaviors, disturbed bodily processes, etc., applications to retardates, psychotic children and geriatric patients.

Schmidt, G. W., & Ulrich, R. E. Effects of Group Contingent Events upon Classroom Noise. *Journal of Applied Behavior Analysis*, 1969, **2**, 171–179.

The first study investigated a group control procedure for suppression of excessive sound-intensity levels in a regular public school classroom. Reinforcement consisted of a 2-min addition to the class gym period and a 2-min break after maintenance of an unbroken 10-min quiet period as monitored on a decibel meter. Transgressions of the sound limit (42 decibels) resulted in a delay of reinforcement by the resetting of the time to the full 10-min interval. The results indicated that these procedures were highly effective in suppression and control of sound intensities. The second experiment utilized a similar procedure coupled with a procedure of eliminating out-of-seat behavior. Experiment III studied the effects of Exp. II procedures on a single student's out-of-seat behavior rate. All procedures were found effective.

Skinner, B. F. *Science and human behavior.* New York: Macmillan, 1953.

A pioneering statement of how scientific principles of learning and behavior can explain the behavior of humans in a variety of contexts. The book is divided into a part that presents the experimental analysis of behavior and a part that describes how this analysis furthers our understanding of emotions, self-control, thinking, groups, government and law, religion, psychotherapy, education, and economics. The book is written simply and does not require previous training in psychology.

Skinner, B. F. Operant Behavior. *American Psychologist*, 1963, **18**, 503–515.

A discussion by America's foremost contemporary behaviorist of some of the technical, theoretical and methodological aspects of operant conditioning; emphasizes the central importance of contingencies of reinforcement as an explanatory basis for much of the behavior of organisms.

Smith, J. M., & Smith, D. E. P., *Child management: A program for parents*. Ann Arbor, Mich.: Ann Arbor Publishers (610 So. Forest St.), 1966.

A self-instructional manual and guide for parents, teachers and others who deal with children. Although based on principles of operant conditioning, there is a complete absence of academic or theoretical discussions. Instead, the material is organized in terms of 176 problem situations involving: Tantrums, enforcement of rules, eating, sleeping, tasks and responsibilities, development of independence, etc. The manual is designed to help adults handle these and other problems in child management.

Stuart, R. B. Operant-Interpersonal Treatment for Marital Discord. *Journal of Consulting and Clinical Psychology*, 1969, **33**, 675–682.

Discusses the successful application of behavior modification procedures in marriage counseling with four couples who were considering divorce. Each couple was seen for seven sessions over a ten-week period. Major procedures included: (1) Marital discord was explained as problems in interpersonal behavior rather than intrapsychic illness; (2) behaviors to be accelerated in each spouse were specified and frequency recorded; and (3) each spouse provided regular reinforcements of desired behaviors in the other.

Thomas, E. J. (Ed.) *The socio-behavioral approach and applications to social work*. New York: Council on Social Work Education, 1967.

Papers presented at the 1967 Annual Program Meeting of the Council on Social Work Education concerned with the application of socio-behavioral approaches in social work education and practice. Topics include: Principles of behavior modification, applications to social casework, group treatment of children, administrative practice, community organization, and socio-behavioral technology. Of particular relevance and value to the social work profession.

Ullmann, L. P., & Krasner, L. (Eds.) *Case studies in behavior modification*. New York: Holt, Rinehart, & Winston, 1965.

Survey of recent developments and applications of behavior modification; consists of an extensive collection of articles dealing with: Severely disturbed behaviors (13 papers); various neurotic behaviors (10 papers); deviant behaviors in children (13 papers); deviant behaviors in adults (7 papers) and mentally retarded (7 papers). In addition to some fifty articles, this book contains a 63-page Introductory Section on "What Is Behavior Modification?"

334

Ullmann, L. P., & Krasner, L. *A psychological approach to abnormal behavior*. New York: Prentice-Hall, 1969.

This volume of nearly 700 pages provides an introduction to the field of abnormal psychology entirely within the framework of behavioral analysis and modification. It is the first systematic attempt to encompass the essential subject matter of the mental health disciplines on an exclusively behavioral basis. While the traditional psychiatric classification of abnormal behaviors is followed, e.g., the neuroses, psychoses, sociopathic disorders, psychophysiological reactions, situational personality maladjustments, sexual deviations, addictions, behavior disorders in children, mental retardation, etc., all of these disturbances are analyzed and interpreted and their modification discussed strictly in terms of a behavioral model, operant and classical conditioning, behavior modification, behavior therapy and related concepts and procedures. Approximately 1450 references.

Ulrich, R., Stachnik, T., & Mabry, J. (Eds.) *Control of human behavior*. Glenview, Ill.: Scott, Foresman, Vol. I, 1966; Vol. II, 1969.

A collection of readings concerned generally and specifically with the modification of human behavior. Intended for a wide range of readers and to have sufficient flexibility to be useful in a variety of types and levels of training in the behavioral sciences and mental health. Major discussions center around: (1) The scientific analysis of behavior; (2) applications of behavior modification in educational settings, in social relations, in disordered and severely disordered behaviors; (3) fallacies in the interpretation and control of behavior; and (4) implications and prospects of behavior modification.

Ulrich, R., Wolfe, M., & Bluhm, M. Operant Conditioning in the Public Schools. *Educational technology monographs*, I, No. 1, 1968. (Available from Dr. Roger Ulrich, Department of Psychology, Western Michigan University, Kalamazoo, Michigan 49001.)

Concerned with helping teachers function as "experts" in dealing with behavioral problems of elementary school children who would ordinarily be referred to outside agencies for treatment because of disruptive, destructive and other deviant behaviors. Describes inservice training programs for teachers in learning how to use behavior modification techniques and discusses the initial resistance and objections of teachers to such techniques. Also describes applications to a pre-school group in which children two to four years of age learn basic skills in reading, writing and arithmetic.

Valett, R. E. *Modifying children's behavior: A guide for parents and professionals*. 2165 Park Boulevard, Palo Alto, Calif., Fearon Publishers, 1969.

This manual was written as an aid to help parents deal with their children's problems. A variety of problems are presented together with possible solutions and applications of behavioral principles. The material can be used by parents for their own instruction; with individual parent counseling; with parent education groups; and with inservice training for teachers. Includes a number of techniques, aids, etc., that can be utilized and applied by parents, teachers, and others.

Wagner, M. K. Parent Therapists: An Operant Conditioning Method. *Mental Hygiene,* 1968, **52,** 452–455.

Discusses the procedures involved in an outpatient setting in which parents are trained to carry out behavior modification therapy with their own children. A specific case is used to illustrate the process and an outline guide of Reinforcement Procedures for Parents is included.

Wahler, R. G. & Erickson, M. Child Behavior Therapy: A Community Program in Appalachia. *Behaviour Research and Therapy,* 1969, **7,** 71–78.

Describes a community program based on reinforcement therapy involving the use of volunteer workers as child behavior therapists in home and school settings. This program was developed in a psychological clinic of a county health center located in Appalachia where there was widespread poverty, unemployment, welfare needs and low education levels; 95% of the referrals to the clinic were children. Effectiveness of the program over a two-year period is discussed and shows that with adequate consultation from mental health professionals, non-professional personnel can learn to use behavior modification in working with various behavior problems in children.

Wahler, R. G., Winkel, G. H., Peterson, R. E., & Morrison, D. C. Mothers as Behavior Therapists for their Own Children. *Behaviour Research and Therapy,* 1965, **3,** 113–124.

Deviant behaviors in three children were modified by producing specific changes in the behaviors of their mothers which, in turn, produced marked changes in the children. These mothers were able effectively to carry out behavior modification procedures with their own children.

Walder, L. O., Cohen, S. I., Breiter, D. E., Warman, F. C., Orme-Johnson, D., & Pavey, S. Parents as Change Agents. Pre-publication paper, 1969. (Available from Dr. Leopold O. Walder, Department of Psychology, American University, Washington, D.C. 20016).

Discusses results of work with over 50 families in which the parents of children with a variety of deviant behaviors were helped to "treat" their own children through an operant consultation system. Results were generally positive and led the authors to conclude that this kind of parental consultation approach could make a substantial contribution to meeting the mental health manpower problem by helping those who are most closely involved with children (i.e. parents) to do a better job.

Ward, M. H., & Baker, B. L. Reinforcement Therapy in the Classroom. *Journal of Applied Behavior Analysis,* 1968, **I,** 323–328.

Teachers were trained in the systematic use of attention and praise to reduce the disruptive classroom behavior of four first-grade children. Observation measures showed a significant improvement from baseline to treatment for these children and no significant changes for same-class controls. While the amount of teacher attention to target children remained the same from baseline to treatment, the proportion of attention to task-relevant behavior of these children increased. Psychological tests revealed no adverse changes after treatment.

Wasik, B. H., Senn, K., Welch, R. H., & Cooper, B. A. Behavior Modification with Culturally Deprived School Children: Two Case Studies. *Journal of Applied Behavior Analysis*, 1969, **2,** 181–194.

Techniques of behavior modification were employed with two second-grade Negro girls in a demonstration school for culturally deprived children to increase the girls' appropriate classroom behaviors. A classification system that provided for continuous categorization of behavior was used to code the children's behavior in two classroom situations. Data were also taken on the type, duration, and frequency of the teachers' verbal interactions. The study included four conditions: Baseline, Modification I, Postmodification, and Modification II. The treatment variable was positive social reinforcement—Attention and approval contingent upon desirable classroom behaviors—which was presented, withheld, or withdrawn (time-out from social reinforcement). Withholding of social reinforcement was contingent upon inappropriate attention-getting behaviors. Time-out from social reinforcement was contingent upon behaviors classified as aggressive and resistive. After 25 days of Modification I, desirable behavior increased markedly for each girl. The teachers were then asked to return to their Baseline level of performance.

Werry, J. S., & Wollersheim, J. P. Behavior Therapy with Children: A Broad Overview. In S. Chess and A. Thomas (Eds.), *Annual progress in child psychiatry and child development*. New York: Brunner-Mazel, 1968, Chapter 23, pp. 356–378.

Contrasts behavior therapy with traditional approaches, outlines basic principles and techniques of behavior therapy, and covers applications to a variety of disturbances in children.

Wolf, M., Risley, T., Johnston, M., Harris, F., & Allen, E. Application of Operant Conditioning Procedures to the Behavior Problems of an Autistic Child: A Follow-up and Extension. *Behaviour Research and Therapy*, 1967, **5,** 103–111.

Report on the successful treatment over a three-year period of a $3\frac{1}{2}$-year-old autistic boy with deviant behaviors and physical handicaps. This case was first reported in the literature in 1963 and represents one of the earlier demonstrations of the effectiveness of operant procedures.

Wolpe, J. *The practice of behavior therapy*. New York: Pergamon Press, 1969.

Issued in paperback and hardcover, this manual presents in detail the rationale, technical procedures, and results of the behavior therapy methods developed by the author. The emphasis is on the methods he has popularized—systematic desensitization and assertive training. It is both a "how-to-do-it" manual and a comprehensive introduction to the field. It gives inadequate attention to methods stemming from the operant conditioning tradition.

Wolpe, J., & Lazarus, A. A. *Behavior therapy techniques*. New York: Pergamon Press, 1966.

This book was written primarily as a practical introduction to the principles and techniques of behavior therapy as developed and practiced by the authors. The framework is that of Pavlovian and Hullian learning principles, rather than operant conditioning, and includes emphasis on such concepts and techniques as desensitization, extinction, reciprocal inhibition, relaxation responses, assertive responses, sexual responses, hypnosis, and aversive conditioning.

Yates, A. J. *Behavior therapy*. New York: Wiley, 1970.

This up-to-date survey of behavior therapy is divided into an excellent historical section, a section on techniques, and a critical examination of the results of behavior therapy. Techniques are described for the treatment of enuresis, stuttering, phobias, obsessions and compulsions, hysterias, tics, sexual disorders, delinquency, psychoses, alcoholism and drug addiction, and mental deficiency.

Zeilberger, J., Sampen, S. E., & Sloane, H. N., Jr. Modification of a Child's Problem Behaviors in the Home with the Mother as Therapist. *Journal of Applied Behavior Analysis*, 1968, **1,** 47–53.

The case of a $4\frac{1}{2}$-year-old boy with deviant behaviors, including screaming, fighting, kicking, hitting, demanding, and related destructive behaviors. This boy's college-educated parents had been unable to manage him and had been told by the family doctor that his behavior reflected "a severe emotional problem." The mother was instructed in how to use systematic reinforcement contingencies and time-out procedures in the home to bring about marked decreases in destructive, and increases in desirable, behaviors.

JOURNALS

Journals that are primarily devoted to the publication of research, applications, reports, and discussions concerned with behavioral analysis and modification are listed below:

Behavior Modification Monographs
New publication currently available under the title of Educational Technology Monographs, Box 1066,
Kalamazoo, Michigan 49001

Behavior Therapy
Journal of the Association for Advancement of Behavior Therapy
Academic Press
111 Fifth Avenue
New York, N.Y. 10003

Behaviour Research and Therapy
Pergamon Press
Maxwell House, Fairview Park
Elmsford, New York 10523

Journal of Applied Behavior Analysis
Department of Human Development
University of Kansas
Lawrence, Kansas 66044

Journal of Behavior Therapy and Experimental Psychiatry
Pergamon Press
Maxwell House, Fairview Park
Elmsford, New York 10523

School Applications of Learning Theory
Kalamazoo Valley Intermediate School District
Box 2025
Kalamazoo, Michigan 49003

INDEX

HUMAN GROWTH AND THE DEVELOPMENT OF PERSONALITY, 2nd Rev. Ed.

Mental Health and Social Medicine

By **Dr. Jack H. Kahn,** *Community Psychiatrist and Medical Director of the Child Guidance Clinic, London Borough of Newham, England*

The second fully revised edition of this highly successful text deals with physical, intellectual, and emotional aspects of the life cycle from infancy to old age concurrently with the social and cultural background. The author has included chapters on adolescence and infantile sexuality.

CONTENTS: Human Needs. Definitions of Personality. Developmental Stages. The Suckling. Toilet Training. Infantile Sexuality. The Oedipal Situation. Rejection Acceptance: The Basis of Infant Care. Deprivation and Provision: Separation and Union. The Importance of Play. Social Problems of Education. Primary Education. The Secondary School Child. Adolescence. Courtship and Marriage. Adult Life. Middle Age. Old Age.

1972   **SBN 08-015818-8 (hardbound)**
                                    SBN 08-015817-X (softcover)

THE EFFECTS OF PSYCHOTHERAPY

International Series of Monographs in Experimental Psychology, Volume 15

By **S. Rachman,** *Institute of Psychiatry, University of London*

This book is a comprehensive, critical review of the evidence for the effects of psychotherapy and its value in treating psychiatric patients. Dr. Rachman examines the occurrence and nature of the many spontaneous improvements which occur in psychological disorders, analyzes the disputed therapeutic claims for psychoanalysis, reviews research into the changes produced by psychotherapy, and traces the growth of behavioral treatments to their current status.

1972   **SBN 08-016805-1 (hardbound)**
                                    SBN 08-016807-8 (softcover)

THE PSYCHIATRIC PROGRAMMING OF PEOPLE: Neo-Behavioral Orthomolecular Psychiatry
By **H.L. Newbold, M.D.**

Using the cybernetic model of the computer, this volume is an attempt to integrate the behavioral aspects of life with the biochemical base upon which all living creatures exist. The book is based on the author's premise that man is, for psychological purposes, a computer, and that this computer can fail to function properly if the hardware (central nervous system) is physically or chemically damaged or if the software (Biologically Programmed Computer or Socially Programmed Computer) is abnormal. This is not a "how-to" book for psychiatry, but rather is an orientation encompassing all forms of treatment, from electroshock therapy to psychoanalysis, binding them all into a single, unified theory of personality and therapy.

1972   PGPS-25   SBN 08-016791-8

COLLEGE AND STUDENT
Selected Readings in the Social Psychology of Higher Education
Edited by **Kenneth A. Feldman,** *State University of New York at Stony Brook*

The thirty-two readings that comprise this source book are concerned with the student in college and, in a sense, the college in the student. Focusing on the connections between students' *intra*personal and *inter*personal processes (whether these latter occur in a friendship dyad or among the members of a multiversity of 40,000 students), the selections in **College and Student** include recent, provocative theoretical efforts, scholarly analyses, and reports of recent research.

College and Student will also provide an excellent supplementary textbook for courses in social psychology, socialization, culture and personality, the sociology (psychology) of youth, and the numerous new courses devoted specifically to higher education that are currently being added to college curricula.

**1972   PGPS-28   SBN 08-016785-3 (hardbound)
                                 SBN 08-016788-8 (softcover)**

THE PRACTICE OF BEHAVIOR THERAPY
By **Joseph Wolpe,** *Temple University Medical School*

This volume systematically presents the most recent developments in both the theory and application of behavior therapy techniques. Professor Wolpe focuses on the practical approach to the neurotic personality, viewing the patient in his totality: an organism completely determined by his constitution, his environment, and his learning.

1969   PGPS-1   SBN 08-006563-5 (hardbound)
                          SBN 08-006390-X (softcover)

SMOKING: A BEHAVIORAL ANALYSIS
By **Bernard Mausner** and **Ellen S. Platt,** *both of Beaver College, Glenside, Pennsylvania,* with the assistance of **Judith S. Mausner,** *The Medical College of Pennsylvania*

This detailed report on the psychological aspects of cigarette smoking, based on the thesis that a comprehensive analysis of a particular behavior pattern itself is necessary for understanding the results of any attempts to influence smoking, provides an understanding of the reasons the community at large applies or ignores scientific advances. The volume first describes a series of investigations into the natural history of smoking and analyzes material drawn from interviews, questionnaires, and diaries furnished by adolescent and adult smokers. Questionnaire data from young men on the role of smoking in their lives and their beliefs concerning the consequences of continuing to smoke or stopping were related to measures of personality. The second part of the book records the results of an experiment testing the effect of role playing on smoking behavior.

1971   PGPS-12   SBN 08-016397-1

PSYCHOTHERAPEUTIC ATTRACTION
By **Arnold P. Goldstein,** *Syracuse University, New York*

Encompassing approximately twenty-five integrated investigations conducted over a five-year period, the research program reported in this volume extrapolates the procedures and findings, from social-psychological research on interpersonal attraction to diverse clinical settings, and examines the usefulness of these procedures for enhancing the level of therapist-patient attraction in psychotherapy. The author discusses thoroughly such methods as direct structuring, therapist structuring, trait structuring, modeling, and role playing.

1971   PGPS-14   SBN 08-016398-X

BEHAVIORAL INTERVENTION IN HUMAN PROBLEMS
Edited by **Henry C. Rickard,** *University of Alabama*

Written by experienced psychologists and mental health coordinators, this volume examines a wide range of successful behavior modification programs geared toward improving the status of individuals with problems in personal and social adjustment. Although the programs outlined differ significantly in the population involved—retardates, emotionally disturbed children, severely disturbed mental hospital patients, prison inmates—each emphasizes adaptive, environmental functioning as opposed to "intrapsychic" change and involves a minimum of mental health professional resources.

1971   **PGPS-10**   SBN 08-016327-0

THE QUESTION OF PLAY
Pergamon English Library
By **Joyce McLellan,** *Eastbourne College of Education, England*

This book is an account of theories formulated to explain why children play and how play aids their development. The text shows how parents can create conditions to encourage play. The author emphasizes the importance of play in learning situations. A bibliography is included. CONTENTS: Part I: The Problem Before Us. The Older Theories of Play. Twentieth Century Theories of Play. Play in the Post-War World. Part II: Play in the First Two Years of Life. The Pre-school Child at Play. The Significance of Play in the Infant School. Play in Literature. Conclusion.

1972   SBN 08-006469-8

CLASSROOM MANAGEMENT: The Successful Use of Behavior Modification
By **K. Daniel O'Leary** and **Susan G. O'Leary**, *both of the State University of New York at Stony Brook*

In addition to the material provided by the authors, this volume contains 37 research articles on such varied methods of classroom behavior modification as the systematic use of teacher attention, token reinforcement, punishment, modeling, peers and para-professionals as therapeutic agents, programmed instruction, and self-management. Editorial comments throughout the book discuss the advantages and disadvantages of the various approaches. The last section of the book deals specifically with the ways in which teachers can utilize these research findings in a practical fashion in their classrooms.

1972   PGPS-27   SBN 08-016789-6 (hardbound)
                                 SBN 08-016790-X (softcover)